so pretty! CROCHET

so pretty! CROCHET

Inspiration and Instructions for **24** Stylish Projects

AMY PALANJIAN

STITCH CHARTS BY
RAE RITCHIE

CHRONICLE BOOKS
SAN FRANCISCO

Text copyright © 2012 by Amy Palanjian.
Photographs copyright © 2012 by Alex Farnum.
Charts copyright © 2012 by Rae Ritchie.

Library of Congress Cataloging-in-Publication Data

Palanjian, Amy.
  So pretty! crochet : inspiration and instructions for 24 stylish
 projects / Amy Palanjian ; stitch charts by Rae Ritchie.
    p. cm.
  Includes index.
  ISBN 978-1-4521-0360-0
  1. Crocheting—Patterns. I. Title.
 TT825.P35 2012
 746.43'4041—dc23
                       2011017459

Manufactured in China

Designed by Allison Weiner
Wardrobe styling by Jasmine Hamed
Prop styling by Christine Wolheim
Typesetting by DC Typography Inc.

10 9 8 7 6 5 4 3 2 1

Chronicle Books LLC
680 Second Street
San Francisco, California 94107

www.chroniclebooks.com

Coats & Clark is a registered trademark of Coats & Clark Inc.
DMC is a registered trademark of Dollfus-Mieg & Cie. Flickr is
a registered trademark of Yahoo! Inc. Gingher's is a registered
trademark of Fiskars Brands, Inc. Gutermann is a registered
trademark of Gutermann & Co. Knit One, Crochet Too is
registered trademark of Knit One, Crochet Too, Inc. Liberty of
London is a registered trademark of Liberty Limited Public Co.
Lion Brand is a registered trademark of Orchard Yarn & Thread
Company, Inc. Stiffy is a registered trademark of Plaid Enterprises
Inc. Stitch Nation is a registered trademark of Deborah S. Stoller.
Tencel is a registered trademark of Lenzing Aktiengesellschaft
Public Limited Co. Valdani is a registered trademark of Valdani
Inc. X-ACTO is a registered trademark of Elmer's Products, Inc.
YouTube is a registered trademark of Google Inc.

CONTENTS

INTRODUCTION 8

TOOLS & TECHNIQUES 12

PROJECTS 28

INTRO-
DUCTION

As a magazine editor and avid blog reader, I see hundreds of craft projects, products, and patterns each week. But the ones that catch my eye are the ones that come with a story—a story that explains a bit about the woman behind each handmade item. I love knowing what inspired her to be creative and in what context she explored her craft. Knowing the backstory allows me to connect with both the person and the craft on a more intimate level.

Crochet has benefited greatly from an explosion of women interpreting the craft on their own terms and sharing their stories of creative pursuits. No longer is it only a means to make an afghan, but the essential identity of crochet has expanded. It's now a way to make intricate jewelry, including necklaces, bracelets, and rings, using leather and thread as delicate as lace. It's a means to create personal accessories, like mittens and hats, using the finest cashmere worked with an eye on the smallest details. It's also a method to create home accessories like pillows, rugs, and bowls, using repurposed materials, reinterpreted patterns, and improvised techniques. In fact, crochet

has gone so far from the stuffy image it had a few decades ago that at first glance, you might not even realize that some of the projects in this book are made with a crochet hook.

More importantly, though, for a growing community of women all over the world, exploring crochet with their own unique perspectives is a way to take knowledge that's been handed down—whether from a grandmother, an aunt, an online friend, or even a trusted book—and distill it according to their own preferences. So at the same time that the projects in this book give a nod to traditions and shared learning, there is a decided leaning forward, a stretching of the basic idea of crochet into something more inclusive and interesting.

The innovation in this one category of craft speaks to our growing need to balance our modern, busy lives with physical handiwork. More and more of us feel a deep need to make things with our hands in order to feel grounded in the rest of our lives. It helps us to feel a sense of accomplishment—to calm our minds with deliberate (and often repetitive and soothing) work. Considered this way, the act of sitting down to crochet a new necklace or a table runner is almost an act of self-preservation. And increasingly, it's a way to show the world who we are and what we're capable of—on our own creative terms.

In this book, you'll find a mix of projects that demonstrate these ideas. The twelve contributors—from countries around the world, including the United States, Portugal, Latvia, Cyprus, and Australia—each offer up two incredibly unique crochet projects that show off their personalities and individual skills. They include jewelry like a looped necklace, stacked leather rings, a lariat, and a cuff bracelet; home accessories including nesting bowls, ornaments, a pillow cover, and bunting; and personal accessories such as scalloped wristlets, mittens, a sweet hat, a darling pouch, and much, much more. The range of projects will give you room to play with new skills, explore new ideas, and entertain your own creative sparks. To me, this diversity in the interpretation of crochet is truly inspiring, so go, turn the page, crochet yourself some treats, and enjoy learning from these incredibly crafty women.

—*Amy*

TOOLS & TECHNIQUES

Crochet is a craft that involves relatively few supplies. Stock up on quality notions and tools, and you'll have them for years to come.

EMBROIDERY THREAD

Often made with six strands woven together, embroidery thread is used to embellish projects or to work very fine crochet. It is also known as embroidery floss and is available in cotton, linen, metallic, and rayon.

HOOKS

The basic tool for crochet comes in plastic, bamboo, and aluminum, and choosing your preferred material is really up to you since each feels slightly differently in hand. The lower the number, the smaller the hook, and the thinner the thread or yarn that you will use with it. Higher-numbered hook sizes are usually used with thicker yarns. Here are the standard sizes in letter, number, and millimeter (mm), which may or may not all appear on a yarn or thread label—it depends on where you live and the manufacturer. (Though there will always be at least one measurement for your reference.)

Size B/1/2.25 mm
Size C/2/2.75 mm
Size D/3/3.25 mm
Size E/4/3.5 mm
Size F/5/3.75 mm
Size G/6/4 mm or 4.25 mm
Size 7/4.5 mm
Size H/8/5 mm
Size I/9/5.5 mm
Size J/10/6 mm

Size K/10.5/6.5 mm
Size L/11/8 mm
Size M/13/9 mm
Size N/15/10 mm
Size P/16/11.5 mm
Size Q/19/16 mm
Size R/27/17 mm
Size S/35/19 mm
Size T/42/22 mm
Size U/50/25 mm
Size V/28 mm

Note: There are also tiny steel hooks that are used for projects with more intricate stitches. They have their own numbering system, which runs from Size 00 (3.5 mm; the largest) through Size 14 (.75 mm; the smallest). Measurements can vary, so pay most attention to the mm called for to avoid the otherwise inevitable confusion.

SCISSORS

A pair of small scissors will suffice for most projects and will fit into any portable sewing kit. Gingher's 4- or 5-inch Knife-Edge Embroidery Scissors come with a protective cover for safe storage and are sharp enough to prevent your yarn from fraying when you snip (available at gingher.com). A pair of blunt-edge baby scissors (available at most drugstores) is also a safe option for crocheters with kids (or pets) around.

SEWING THREAD

Since some inexpensive sewing thread breaks easily due to poor quality, look for cotton or hand-quilting thread by Guetermann, or cotton-covered polyester Button & Craft thread by Coats & Clark. Both are strong and durable options.

TAPESTRY NEEDLE

This type of needle is thick with a big eye, which is helpful for threading thicker yarns when it's time to weave in your ends or sew pieces of a project together.

COMMON ABBREVIATIONS

approx = approximately

beg = begin or beginning

CC = contrast color

ch = chain stitch(es)

ch-sp = space previously made

dc = double crochet

dec = decrease(s)(ing)

hdc = half double crochet

inc = increase(es)(ing)

MC = main color

rep = repeat(s)(ing)

rnd(s) = round(s)

RS = right side

rsc = reverse single crochet

sc = single crochet

sc2tog = single crochet 2 together

sk = skip

sl = slip

sl st = slip stitch

sp(s) = space(s)

st(s) = stitch(es)

t-ch = turning chain

tbl = through back loop

tr = treble/triple crochet

WS = wrong side

yo = yarn over

Here are the most common terms that you will come across as you crochet, along with a breakdown of stitches.

BLOCKING

Blocking is the act of dampening a finished project to gently work it into the desired shape as it dries. It can be used to even out stitches in a finished item. Check the care instructions on your yarn before blocking—acrylics should not be steam blocked.

Spray Blocking

Lay your item on a clean, dry towel on a flat surface. Use a spray bottle to mist with room-temperature water. Gently pull the item into the desired shape. When done, allow your item to air dry, pinning it to a blocking board if desired.

Steam Blocking

Place your item on a clean, dry towel on a flat surface. Place a cool, wet washcloth on top and heat your iron to the setting that corresponds to the fiber of your yarn (which you can find on the yarn label). Press the iron on the washcloth for a few seconds to create steam. Gently coerce your item into the proper shape while steaming and repeat steaming (and rewetting the washcloth) as needed. When done, allow your item to air dry, pinning it to a blocking board (available at yarn.com) if desired.

Wet Blocking

Wash your item according to the instructions on your yarn label. Lay the item flat on a clean towel and then roll it up in the towel, pressing out water as you go. Repeat this with dry towels until the item is mostly dry. Then, on a flat, clean surface, lay out your item and pull it into the desired size and shape. When done, allow your item to air dry, pinning it to a blocking board if desired.

CHAIN STITCH (ch)

Holding the hook in your right hand, loop the yarn (from the ball) over your left index finger. Hold the end of the yarn between your left thumb and middle finger. Use your left index finger to wrap the yarn from back to front around the body of the hook, then use the hook to pull the yarn through the loop. With the yarn on the hook, one chain is made. Repeat making chains as directed by your pattern, but don't count your slipknot or the loop on your hook as a stitch. This row of stitches is the foundation of your project. (A chain stitch is also used to make spaces and loops in your yarn.)

DECREASE(S)(ING) (dec)

Often, you'll be directed to decrease stitches to taper a project (like gloves). The most common way to do this is to single crochet two stitches together.

DOUBLE CROCHET (dc)

About twice the height of a single crochet stitch, a double crochet is much looser than a single crochet.

DYE LOT

This is the batch that the yarn was dyed in, which means that all of the yarn in one batch will be exactly the same color (the lot number is usually indicated on the label). When buying yarn for a project, be sure to buy enough of the same dye lot to complete it—especially with hand-dyed yarn—to ensure that all of your yarn is the same exact color.

FASTENING OFF

When you finish a project or part of a project, you'll have to secure the yarn so that the stitches don't unravel. Cut the yarn off the ball, leaving a few inches hanging. Use your hook to draw the cut end of the yarn through the loop on your hook, then remove the hook and pull the end of the yarn to secure it. Use a yarn needle to weave the end of the yarn through the end row of stitches to hide it. Even out the tension after each time you fasten off.

FOUNDATION CHAIN

The first row of chain stitches is the foundation chain. You will build the project off of this chain.

GAUGE

Gauge is the proper tension you should work to make sure that your crocheted piece will be the right size when it's completed. You may need to change hook size in order to work at the given gauge if you are not using the exact yarn called for in a pattern. This is most important when making garments or anything that you would like to fit exactly, and less important with other projects like ornaments. Gauge is usually defined in a pattern by a ratio of stitches and rows to a given measurement. You should test a small 4-by-4-in/10-by-10-cm swatch of fabric in the stitch pattern of the piece you plan to make before starting the project. Count the number of stitches and rows in the measurement designated by the gauge given in the pattern. If you find that your swatch has more stitches and rows than the gauge, you are working too tightly and will want to change to a larger hook (or try to loosen up your stitches). If you have fewer stitches and rows, you are working too loosely and will want to change to a smaller hook (or tighten up your stitches). Keep changing hook size until you arrive at the proper gauge.

GRIP

There are two basic ways to hold a crochet hook. The first is as you would hold a pencil, between your thumb and index finger. The other option is to hold the hook like a knife, placing your right hand over it, grasping it between your thumb and index finger. Choose whichever way feels best to you.

HALF DOUBLE CROCHET (hdc)

This stitch is just what it sounds like—halfway, in height, between a single and a double crochet stitch.

JOINING A NEW BALL OF YARN

When you're about to run out of yarn, which will inevitably happen on larger projects, work your last stitch until there are two loops left on your hook. Leaving a tail, draw the end of the new yarn through the two loops, then continue working with the new ball of yarn. With a large-eyed needle, weave in the tails of both balls of yarn to secure without tying a knot. You can also use this method when you want to join or switch to a different color.

REVERSE SINGLE CROCHET (rsc)

This is just like normal single crochet except that you'll be going left to right (instead of right to left). If a reverse single crochet is called for at the end of a single crochet row, twist your wrist and insert the crochet hook back into the last stitch you made instead of turning your work. Work a single crochet and continue the row.

ROUND(S)

A round is a single row of your crochet stitches worked in a circle, as with a hat or a bowl, that is either joined at each round end or worked as a spiral.

ROW

A single row of your crochet stitches as worked in a straight line is one row. In most cases, you will turn a piece at the end of a row and continue working back in the opposite direction.

SIMPLE INVISIBLE SEAMING

The easiest way to join two pieces of crochet—like two granny squares—is to simply sew them together. Place the two pieces together, right sides facing, matching stitches across the edges. Thread a needle with a length of yarn and use it to weave the yarn through a few inches (or centimeters) on an adjacent side to one that is about to be joined together to anchor the end. Bring the needle out at the corner where you plan to join the two pieces together in preparation for sewing. Do not make a knot. Insert your needle through the corner of the opposite piece and draw the yarn through. Insert your needle through the next row-end stitch on the first piece and draw the yarn through. Continue to sew up the seam, working in a zigzag pattern for the length of the seam. At the end, weave the yarn through several stitches to anchor it on an adjacent edge, then cut the tail.

SINGLE CROCHET (sc)

This is the most basic stitch and it is the base of every other stitch. To make a single crochet stitch, make your starting chain plus one more than the number of single crochet stitches called for in the pattern. Put your hook, from the front to the back, into the center of the second chain from the hook. (You will have two loops on your hook now.) Yarn over by wrapping the yarn from the back to the front around your hook. Pull the yarn through the chain with your hook (there will be two loops on the hook). Yarn over again and then pull two loops through on your hook to complete one single crochet. Place the hook in the center of your next chain stitch and yarn over. Pull the yarn through the stitch, yarn over, and pull the yarn through the two loops that are on your hook. Keep repeating to the end of your foundation chain.

Start the second row by first turning your work and chain one (don't count the chain as a stitch). Place your hook under the top two loops of your first single crochet in the row below, from front to back. Yarn over and pull the yarn through the stitch. Yarn over and pull the yarn through the two loops that are on your hook to complete a single crochet. Repeat for each single crochet across your row.

SINGLE CROCHET SEAM

Just like a slip stitch seam, but with single crochet stitches in place of the slip stitches.

SINGLE CROCHET 2 TOGETHER (sc2tog)

This is a common way to decrease stitches to make an item smaller by using single crochet stitches to join two stitches together. Insert your hook into a stitch and draw up a loop. Insert your hook into the next stitch and draw up another loop. Yarn over and draw all three loops onto the hook.

SKIP (sk)

A direction to skip means to skip the next stitch. A direction to skip two means that you should skip the next two stitches.

SLIPKNOT

To start any crochet project, you'll need to make a slipknot. Pull the yarn strand from the center of the ball and make a loop about 6 in/15 cm from the end by placing the tail of the yarn in front of the ball yarn. Let the rest of the tail yarn fall slightly behind the loop. Put your hook into the loop and scoop up the yarn in the back of the loop with the hook. Pull it through the front of the loop and gently pull the tail yarn to tighten the loop around the hook. The slipknot does not count as a stitch unless specified.

SLIP STITCH SEAM

Align two pieces, like two granny squares, right sides facing, lining up the stitches that you intend to join. Make a slipknot with your yarn and then put your hook through the first stitch of both pieces. Pull it through the slip stitch, and insert your hook through the next stitch of both pieces. Yarn over, drawing the yarn through both stitches and loop on hook, all in one motion. Continue across edge to complete the seam. Even out the tension and then fasten off.

TREBLE/TRIPLE CROCHET (tr)

To make a triple crochet, which is a bit taller than a double crochet, make a starting chain with three more chains than the number of triple crochet stitches that the pattern calls for. Skip the first four chain stitches—they count as the turning chain—and yarn over your hook twice. Put your hook from front to back into the center of the fifth chain from the hook. Yarn over, pulling the yarn through the chain (four loops will now be on the hook). Yarn over, pulling the yarn through two loops on your hook (three loops will be on your hook). Yarn over, pulling the yarn through two loops on your hook (two loops will be on your hook). Yarn over, pulling through two loops on your hook, to complete one triple crochet.

Next, yarn over twice and insert your hook into the center of the next chain. Yarn over, pulling the yarn through your stitch. Yarn over again, pulling the yarn through two loops on your hook three times. Repeat to the end of the foundation chain.

To begin the second row, turn your work and chain four for the turning chain. Skip the first triple crochet below the turning chain. Yarn over twice and insert your hook from front to back under the top two loops of the next triple crochet in the row below. Yarn over, drawing the yarn through two loops three times to complete another triple crochet stitch. Repeat this step in each triple crochet across the row and in the top of the turning chain at the end of the row.

TURNING CHAIN (t-ch)
When beginning a row of any stitch, you will be starting at the base of that row. You must start with a turning chain that comes up to the height of your stitches either before or after turning your work. For a single crochet, you need one chain; for half double crochet, you need two chains; for double crochet, you need three chains; and for triple crochet, you need four chains. This will be specified in your pattern.

Usually, the turning chain at the start of a row will take the place of the first stitch. So, after completing the turning chain, you will not make another stitch in the first stitch. You will also work into the turning chain as a stitch when you get to the end of the row.

For single crochet, the turning chain made at the beginning of a single crochet row does not count as a stitch. So after you make your turning chain, you will work a single crochet into the stitch below it (and you won't work in the turning chain on the return row).

TURNING YOUR WORK/TURN
Whenever you reach the end of your work, you'll need to turn it halfway around (clockwise) to be able to start your next row. The last stitch will become the first.

YARN OVER (yo)
This is when you need to bring your yarn around your hook, often in order to increase your stitches.

Learning to crochet is much easier when you watch someone else do it. So ask a friend or family member to teach you, or spend a little time with an online resource. Try videos (which are great because you can stop and start, watching the tricky parts over and over until you understand them) and illustrations to help you through.

BASIC CROCHET STITCHES
(video and illustrations)

* Lionbrand.com: visit the "Learning Center"

* Purlbee.com/crochet-basics: see "Crochet Basics"

* Coatsandclarks.com: look for "Needlecrafts: Crochet How-tos"

* Dmc-usa.com: visit "Learn to Crochet"

GRANNY SQUARES 101
(step-by-step directions for how to make granny squares)

* Meetmeatmikes.blogspot.com

* Purlbee.com/granny-square-project

When following a pattern for a crochet project, you'll be given guidance on what type of yarn is recommended and what size hook to use. Here's a breakdown of what the different fibers you'll see referenced mean.

ACRYLIC

Acrylic yarns are man-made and come in a wide variety of many different weights, colors, and types. The best thing about acrylics is that you can machine wash them and they won't run, fade, or shrink.

ALPACA

Alpaca yarn is known for being stronger, warmer, and softer than sheep's wool. It's also hypoallergenic and it can be as fine as cashmere, or thick and bulky.

BAMBOO

Bamboo yarn is often a blend of bamboo fibers and another fiber such as wool. The bamboo fibers add a soft and somewhat silky feel. From a sustainability standpoint, bamboo is a fast-growing fiber that usually doesn't rely on chemical fertilizers to grow.

MERINO WOOL

A high-quality fiber from merino sheep, merino wool is very commonly used in knitting and crochet yarn because it's both warm and it wicks.

ORGANIC COTTON

This type of fiber is grown and spun without the use of pesticides, herbicides, or other chemicals that could be harmful to the environment and/or your health.

RECYCLED COTTON

Recycled cotton is made from cotton fabric pieces that would otherwise be trashed (as in the case of excess fabric left over from the production of T-shirts). Often, the cotton fibers are worked into a blend to increase their usability.

VARIEGATED YARN

This type of yarn includes many shades of one color family, which can create a look of complexity without needing to change skeins of yarn.

WOOL

While wool fibers can feel scratchy simply based on their innate structure, most wool yarns are processed to be smooth, comfortable, and naturally warm against the skin. Woolen yarn, which has a slightly fuzzy surface, is somewhat heavier in weight than worsted wool.

WORSTED WOOL

Lighter than woolen yarns, the fibers of worsted wool are arranged parallel to each other during processing to create a smoother and less bulky surface. This type of wool also wicks and is super warm.

COMMON YARN WEIGHTS

Yarn comes in a variety of weights and it's good to have a basic understanding of the difference before starting a project (or visiting a yarn shop where you might otherwise be understandably tempted by pretty colors). Knowing what weight you need for a project will help ensure that you are successful and that the pattern works as it's meant to.

CATEGORY 1: SUPER FINE

Sock, Fingering, Baby Yarn
A very lightweight yarn that is often used for socks, baby clothes, and other delicate items like lacy scarves and wraps.

UK/Aus approx equivalent: 3 ply, 4 ply, 5 ply, jumper weight

CATEGORY 2: FINE

Sport Weight, Baby Yarn
A lighter weight yarn that is commonly used for baby clothes and lighter blankets. It's usually very soft, which makes it good for adult garments for people with sensitive skin.

UK/Aus approx equivalent: 8 ply

CATEGORY 3: LIGHT

DK, Light Worsted Yarn
Used for baby, lighter weight, or more delicate garments.

UK/Aus approx equivalent: DK (Double Knit)

CATEGORY 4: MEDIUM

Worsted-Weight, Afghan, Aran Yarn
This is the most popular weight for standard knitting and crocheting projects because it's ideal for garments (scarves, hats, gloves, sweaters) and blankets.

UK/Aus approx equivalent: 10 ply, Aran weight

CATEGORY 5: BULKY

Chunky, Craft, Rug Yarn
Bulky weight yarn, which is thicker than worsted; crochets up quickly for projects like throws, wraps, and scarves.

UK/Aus approx equivalent: 13 ply

CATEGORY 6: SUPER BULKY

Bulky, Roving Yarn
This is a very heavy yarn that is about twice as thick as worsted weight yarn.

UK/Aus approx equivalent: 14 ply

PROJECTS

VICTORIA LETEMENDIA KOUPPARIS

LOFOS TALA PAFOS, CYPRUS

Originally from Texas, Victoria was born to Argentinean parents and spent her childhood in colorful Mexico City. Now, she lives in Cyprus, where she helps run the family restaurant with her husband by night and crochets jewelry by day. "I learned to crochet because I was inspired by a beautiful table runner that I saw in a magazine," she explains. "I thought to myself, 'I could probably make that if I would only learn to crochet.' It was a lightbulb moment." She never did get around to making that runner, but she taught herself to crochet sophisticated and original designs by learning one stitch—chain stitch—through online tutorials.

"I had been making loops in different colors, without really knowing what I was going to do with them. Suddenly, when I placed them all together, they looked really nice and I knew I needed to turn them into a necklace," Victoria says.

FIND VICTORIA

Lavenderfield.etsy.com   Thiswayhandmade.blogspot.com   Twitter.com/lavenderfield63

Two slightly different shades of gray create just enough contrast to up the interest on this simply stunning bib necklace. Try it in the colorway shown here, or adjust to suit your liking—though using at least a touch of metallic DMC thread is recommended as it makes a nice highlight.

MATERIALS

Size 4 steel/2 mm crochet hook

DMC Cotton Pearl thread (size 5) in dark gray

Nine 25-by-15-mm oval loops

One 4-by-2.5-cm teardrop loop

Four 10-mm-outer-diameter round metal loops

Four 12-mm-outer-diameter round metal loops

Scissors

DMC Metallic Pearl Cotton thread in dark silver/gray

Sewing needle

Sewing thread in dark gray

Size 11 seed beads in wild berry

Two 20-mm-outer-diameter metal loops in antiqued silver

Pliers (optional)

Approximately 3 ft/1 m 1½-in-/40-mm-wide sheer organza ribbon in burgundy

Sewing thread in burgundy

1 Using your hook and the cotton DMC dark gray thread, sl st around 7 of the oval loops, the teardrop loop, the 10-mm round loops, and 3 of the 12-mm round loops, covering each completely. Cut your thread and tie a double knot on each loop to secure the crochet. Trim excess thread.

2 Rep Step 1 with the metallic DMC thread and the 2 remaining oval loops and the 1 remaining 12-mm round loop.

3 When you have your loops completed, place them ch st facing up, on a flat work surface according to the design shown on page 32.

4 Start sewing them together with your needle and gray sewing thread, stitching on the backside as neatly as you can. Sew your seed beads on, 1 bead per stitch, in small clusters between the loops, reserving a few for the ribbon. Knot off after each cluster. This completes your bib.

5 Open the 2 antiqued silver metal loops (20-mm outer diameter), using pliers if necessary, and hook them onto either side of the bib. Close them securely.

6 Cut the organza ribbon in half. Take one half, pass it through 1 of the silver loops and fold about ½ in/13 mm under itself.

7 Use your sewing needle and burgundy thread to sew a few seed beads on the organza ribbon, gathering it as you sew. Rep on the other side with the remaining half of ribbon to finish. Tie on to wear.

VARIATIONS

* Arrange your loops in any abstract pattern that you like, adapting the bib to suit your fancy.

* Add more beading than is shown here for a more sparkly version.

* Simplify by using just one size of loop.

Once you nail the method of slip stitching around the metal loops, you can whip out this whimsical necklace in no time. The combination of pretty pastel colors allows this necklace to work splendidly with both a plain white tee and jeans, or a dressy black shift, depending on your day. Choose any color combination you desire.

MATERIALS

Size 4 steel/2 mm crochet hook

Assortment of cotton DMC embroidery thread in pastel colors

Thirty-four 10-mm-outer-diameter round metal loops

Scissors

Two 14- to 15-mm glass flower beads in pastel green
(available from lustrousthings.etsy.com)

3 ft/1 m ⅜-in-/10-mm-wide satin ribbon in gray

1 Using your hook and assorted colors of cotton DMC thread, sl st around the loops, covering each completely. Cut your thread and tie a double knot on each loop to secure the crochet. Trim excess thread.

2 Thread your ribbon through 1 of the glass flower beads, then through all of the loops. Thread the other glass flower bead at the other end.

3 Tie a double knot on either side of the bead to secure the loops and beads in place. To wear, tie on the necklace at the length you like.

VARIATIONS

* Use bigger loops to make a bolder statement.

* Try a monochromatic color palette for a subtler end result.

* Make two necklaces, of varying lengths, to make a double-strand version.

JANELLE
HASKIN

BENSALEM, PENNSYLVANIA

With formal training as an illustrator, Janelle learned to crochet and knit years ago from her grandmother. When she recently decided to make all of her holiday gifts, she picked up a crochet hook again and whipped up neck warmers for her friends. "My favorite pieces have been the ones that have been mistakes," Janelle says of her work, adding that the Scalloped-Edge Neck Warmer (page 41) actually started as a hat that got out of control. She finds loads of inspiration in fashion magazines, in the seasons, and in the texture of different natural materials.

"What I love most about crocheting is that it starts off as a simple skein of yarn, and it's up to you to turn it into something someone will love," notes Janelle.

FIND JANELLE

Janellehaskin.etsy.com   Janellehaskin.blogspot.com   Twitter.com/Jannierox

Chunky and oversized, this piece is a bold statement that will keep you cozy and looking pulled together. The decorative scallops and round shape elevate it above a basic scarf, making it an accessory that deserves to be worn indoors and out.

MATERIALS

2 skeins (6 oz/170 g and 106 yd/97 m) Lion Brand Wool-Ease
Super Bulky Thick & Quick in Fisherman

Size S/35/19 mm crochet hook

Scissors

1 To start making the scalloped edging, ch 41 and join with a sl st to form a ring, being careful not to twist chain.

2 Ch 3 (counts as first dc), dc 5 times in the sl st join of the first ch from Step 1, sl st in next ch—first scallop completed.

3 Sc 1 in next ch.

4 [Dc 6 times in the next ch, sl st in next ch]—next scallop completed, sc 1 in the next ch.

5 Rep Step 4 until you have completed 15 scallops, ending the last scallop with a sl st into base of the first scallop.

6 Make another sl st through the ch in the ring of first scallop.

7 Flip the ring of scallops right-side up and bring the crochet hook and yarn through the ring.

8 Moving on to the body of the neck warmer, ch 1 and sc in every chain until you complete the rnd. (41 sc) Finish with a sl st in the first ch-1 of this step.

9 Ch 3 (counts as first dc), then complete 10 rnds of dc.

10 Ch 1, then do 1 rnd of sc (sc in each dc top).

11 Finish with a sl st in the beginning of sc round, fasten off, and weave in any loose ends.

VARIATIONS

* Make these two-tone by crocheting the scallops in a slightly different shade than the body of the neck warmer.

* Simplify by skipping the scallops and start with Step 8 to make the body of the neck warmer with a basic chain stitch.

* Add an embellishment to one side of the front to dress it up. Try a vintage brooch or a silk or crocheted flower.

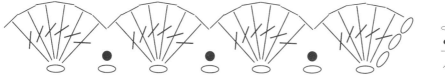

KEY

◦ chain
● slip
⊤ double crochet

A simplified version of fingerless gloves, these wristlets will remind you of playing dress up. Good news, though: You can crochet up a pair and add a bit of fancy to your everyday—not to mention, stay warmer in the cooler months.

MATERIALS

1 skein (3½ oz/100 g and 155 yd/142 m) Stitch Nation Full o' Sheep 100% Peruvian Wool in Little Lamb

Size G/6/4.25 mm crochet hook

Scissors

1 To start making the scalloped edging, ch 45 and join with a sl st to form a ring, being careful not to twist chain.

2 Ch 3 (counts as first dc), dc 5 times in the sl st join of the first ch from Step 1, sl st in next ch—first scallop completed.

3 Sc 1 in the next ch.

4 Dc 6 times in the next ch, ending with a sl st in following ch to complete the second scallop.

5 Sc in next ch.

6 Rep Steps 4 and 5 until you complete the rnd and you have 15 scallops.

7 Join the ends with a sl st to complete the scalloping.

8 Flip the ring of scallops right-side up and bring the crochet hook and the yarn through the ring.

9 To make the body of the glove, sc 1 in every chain around the ring, working into the remaining loops of the chain.

10 Start dec to make the glove fit your wrist: Draw up a loop in next st. Then again, draw up a loop in the next st. There should now be 3 loops on the hook. Yo the hook. Draw the yarn through all 3 loops on hook. You have now made 1 dec.

11 *[Sc 1 in the next 4 st and dec 1 in the next st.] Rep from * until the rnd is complete. (36 sts)

12 Dec 1 and sc 1 in the next 3 ch and rep until rnd is complete. (28 sts)

13 Sc 1 in all ch around ring and complete with a sl st in the beg ch. Rep 4 times working 5 rounds even in sc, and joining at the end of each rnd.

14 Dec 1 and sc 3 and rep until rnd is complete. (22 sts)

15 Sc 1 into each ch around and complete with a sl st in the beg ch. Rep 5 times, working 6 rnds total.

16 Ch 3 (counts as first dc), then dc in every ch around the ring, joining each rnd. Rep 3 times, working 4 rnds total.

17 Ch 1, sc in each st around, end with a sl st in first st. Fasten off.

Repeat pattern to make your second wristlet.

VARIATIONS

* Make these two-tone by crocheting the scallops in a slightly different shade than the body of the gloves.

* Add extra embellishment by weaving a thin ribbon through the base of each glove, and tie a bow at the top of the wrist.

* Make them into arm warmers by making the base of the glove longer so that it hits mid-forearm.

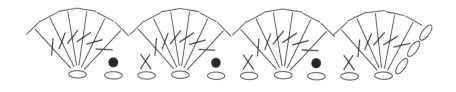

KEY

◯ chain
● slip
✕ single crochet
┬ double crochet

MARGARET OOMEN

ONTARIO, CANADA

As a full-time rural family physician, Margaret Oomen looks to her creative pursuits to balance her work. "Art has become a very important outlet in my life. It is my form of meditation and it keeps me grounded," she explains. After teaching herself how to crochet so that she could make her children hats when they were young, she realized that it's much easier to embellish crocheted items than knitted ones and went on to explore the craft further. "I collected some beautiful smooth stones on a summer vacation to Cape Breton, Nova Scotia, and was inspired to cover a few of them after seeing fishermen's nets," she says. For Margaret, the connection to nature is key: "I love holding the smooth stones in my hands as I work, thinking about their composition, journeys, and places of origin."

"I always try to remember where my inspiration comes from because it helps me remain true to myself," Margaret says.

FIND MARGARET
Knitalatte.etsy.com   Resurrectionfern.typepad.com   Twitter.com/knitalatte

It can be hard to remember that we're all connected—and that we're all connected to nature—through the hustle and bustle of our daily lives, but this stone was designed to celebrate that fact. Keep one (or two) around to help you appreciate the small moments of connection.

MATERIALS

1 approximately 3-in/7½-cm smooth flat stone

108 yd/100 m pearl crochet cotton (such as Valdani, size 12)

Size J/10/6 mm crochet hook

Scissors

Tapestry needle

Rnd 1: Ch 10 and join ch with a sl st to form a circle.

Rnd 2: Ch 5 (counts as first tr 1, ch 1), then *(tr 1, ch 1), and rep from * 11 times (12 tr and 12 ch). Join with a sl st to the fourth ch of beg ch.

Rnd 3: Ch 6 (counts as tr, ch 3), then *(tr 1, ch 3) and rep from * 11 times. Join with a sl st to the fifth ch of beg ch.

Rnd 4: Ch 8 (counts as tr 1, ch 5), *(tr 1, ch 5) and rep from * 11 times. Join with a sl st to the seventh ch of beg ch.

Rnd 5: Ch 11, *(tr 1, ch 8) and rep from * 11 times. Join with a sl st to the tenth ch of beg ch.

Rep the last rnd until the crocheted piece will fit easily over the smooth stone. If you have done this correctly, it will curl slightly inwards and appear like a very shallow basket. Slip your stone inside the basket.

Ch 6, *(sc 1, ch 2) and rep from * 11 times. Join with a sl st to the first loop. Don't be afraid to pull the thread as tightly as possible, as it will give a tighter fit and a more beautiful end result. Fasten off and thread the tail on your needle and sew it invisibly through the last row. Trim the thread and then sew in your starting tail.

VARIATIONS

* Use a few colors of thread to give a more vibrant look to your stone.

* Make a little collection and use them as paperweights on your desk or to decorate the center of a dining table.

* Use a slightly thicker thread or yarn for a wintery variation.

When it's time to clean out your closet, repurpose your T-shirt pile into an extra-soft rag rug. Sort the T-shirts by color to create a balanced color palette, get to crocheting, and consider the finished product an easy way to treat your feet throughout the house.

MATERIALS

Approximately 20 used, clean, adult T-shirts (more if they are small or children's size; estimated yardage total is about 80 to 100 yd/73 to 91 m)

Scissors or rotary cutter and mat

Ruler

Size V/28 mm crochet hook

These instructions will create a rug that's 3 ft/1 m in diameter.

❶ Collect your T-shirts and cut them widthwise into 2-in-/7-cm-wide strips starting at the bottom of each shirt. Lay the strips out on a large surface to decide your color pattern, trying your best to not have the same colored strips side by side.

❷ To join the strips, simply tie them together or use this method: Make a small hole in both ends of the strips that you want to join. Place 1 end of 2 strips on top of each other. Pull the long end of the strip that's on top through the holes of the stacked strips. Pull until the entire strip has gone through and tug gently to secure the joint.

❸ Roll up all your joined strips into a giant rag ball. Now, you're ready to start crocheting.

Join the end of each round before continuing with the following step.

Rnd 1: Ch 5, join with a sl st to form a ring. Dc 5 working around the ch (into the center of the ring), then sl st together to join. (5 dc)

Rnd 2: Begin your inc: Inc by making 2 dc in 1 st and continue to make 2 dc in each st around the circle. (10 dc)

Rnd 3: Continue working in the rnd, making an inc in every second st. In other words, continue inc 5 sts in each rnd.

Rnd 4: Continue working in the rnd, making an inc in every third st.

Rnd 5: Continue working in the rnd, making an inc in every fourth st. Continue following this pattern of increases allowing 1 more st between increases each rnd until you have reached the desired size or the end of your rag ball.

Pull the end through the last st and hide it by weaving it through the last few sts. If it doesn't immediately lie flat, cover it with some heavy books for a day or so.

VARIATIONS

* Make an extra-large rug, working additional increases if the piece starts to cup (curl up at the edges) and use it as the focal point of a room.

* Try using worn (and clean) floral sheets for a more feminine look.

* Use this method with super chunky yarn for a slightly different effect.

BRANDY VELTEN

WILMINGTON, NORTH CAROLINA

While working on her master's degree in marine biology, Brandy fits in crochet around her studies. "My mom always did a lot with her hands, and she's been an all-around inspiration," Brandy says. After a hiatus from crochet, which she did when she was younger, Brandy retaught herself the craft and now focuses on making items that are both stylish and functional. "I definitely approach my items with a 'How will this be used in my customers' lives?' and 'Why would they want to use it?'," she continues. By paying attention to color trends and listening to feedback from her family, Brandy is able to put her own spin on personal accessories including headbands, slippers, and the occasional brooch.

"I can go yarn shopping and have no idea what I plan to make, but by the time I'm done, I always have ideas spinning around my head all due to texture and color," says Brandy.

FIND BRANDY
Brokenhallelujah.etsy.com   Brokenxhallelujah.blogspot.com   Twitter.com/bhallelujah

Forget the headache fear that often comes with the thought of wearing a headband. This soft and adjustable adornment is totally pain free, with cheerfulness guaranteed to perk up any outfit.

MATERIALS

Approximately 19 yd/17 m Caron Simply Soft (shown in Ocean)

Approximately 4 yd/3½ m Caron Simply Soft (shown in Vanilla)

MC (Ocean) will be the headband base and inner
and outer ring of the flower

CC (Vanilla) will be the middle ring of the flower

Size H/8/5 mm crochet hook

Scissors

Tapestry needle

Matching sewing thread (optional)

This pattern contains instructions on how to make an adult-size headband. However, the headband base can be adjusted to fit smaller-sized heads. Keep in mind that the flower is sewn onto the headband base.

HEADBAND

Starting with MC, ch 121 and turn.

Row 1: In second ch from hook, sc 20, ch 80, sk next 80 ch, and sc in last 20 sts. Do not turn. (If needed, adjust the "ch 80" in this row to change the size of the headband. For example, a child's headband for ages 3 to 6 would have approximately ch 70 to 75 instead of ch 80.)

Row 2: Working on the opposite side of the last 20 sc completed in Row 1, sl st in 20 sc, ch 80, sk 80 previous chs, and sl st in last 20 sts. Tie off and weave in ends.

You should now have a linear headband. Each end is the thicker "tie" portion used to tie the headband around the head, with 3 separate chains of 80 in the middle of each end.

FLOWER

Using MC, ch 2 and turn.

Rnd 1: In second ch from hook, sc 12 to form a circle of sts, and sl st to join rnd.

Rnd 2: Ch 3, *[sk 1 sc, sc 1, ch 3]; rep from * around to form 6 loops, sl st into first ch of beg ch-3.

Rnd 3: Using CC, *[sc 1, hdc 1, dc 1, hdc 1, sc 1 in next loop]; rep from * in each ch-3 loop from the previous rnd for a total of 6 petals. Sl st to sc 1 of the first petal.

Rnd 4: Continuing in CC, ch 3, *[in hdc of petal, sc 1, ch 3, sc in sc of same petal, and ch 3]. (Each petal should have a sc in the hdc and the last sc.) Rep from * around to form 12 loops, then sl st in third ch of beg ch-3.

Rnd 5: Using MC, *[sc 1, hdc 1, dc 1, hdc 1, sc 1 in next loop]; rep from * in each ch-3 loop from the previous rnd for a total of 12 petals. Sl st to sc 1 of first petal. Fasten off and weave in ends.

Using MC and the tapestry needle, sew the flower onto the headband base on each of the 3 strands. The flower shown on page 56 is placed about 25 stitches from one edge of the headband.

VARIATIONS

* Make the headband and the flower in the same color.

* Add a decorative button to the center of the flower.

* Make the headband part shorter and use it as a cuff bracelet.

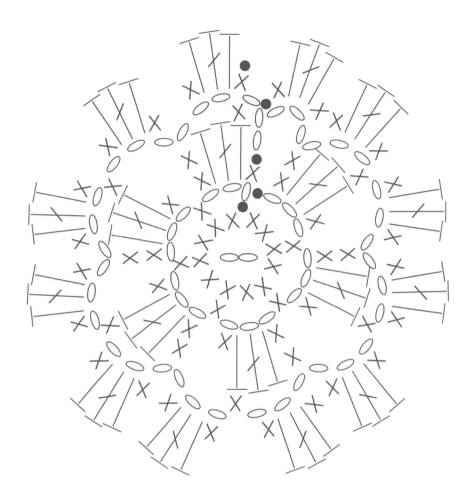

KEY

⬯ chain
● slip
✕ single crochet
╁ half double crochet
┬ double crochet

Sweeter than socks, these soft slippers will inspire a feeling of flirty femininity in you, even when you're padding around the house in sweats. Plus, they are made, by design, to form to your feet.

MATERIALS

Approximately 200 yd/183 m Caron Simply Soft (shown in Ocean)

Approximately 7 yd/6½ m Caron Simply Soft (shown in Vanilla)

MC (Ocean) will be the slipper body

CC (Vanilla) will be the accent color

Size I/9/5.5 mm crochet hook

Scissors

Tapestry needle

Matching sewing thread

Two ¾-in/2-cm buttons

This pattern is done in double crochet starting at the toe and working toward the heel. The front part of the slipper is crocheted in the round. The strap is crocheted last with the edging of the slipper. This pattern is written for size 7 to 10 slippers (37 to 41 Euro); adjust as necessary where noted.

TOE OF SLIPPER

Rnd 1: Using MC, ch 3 and then in the third ch from the hook, hdc 11. (Ch 2 counts as first hdc.) (12 sts)

Rnd 2: Hdc in ch-2 from Rnd 1, hdc 2 in next hdc, *[hdc in next hdc, hdc 2 in next hdc]; rep from * around, ending hdc 2 in the last st of Rnd 1. (18 sts)

Rnd 3: Hdc in each st around. (18 sts)

Rnd 4: Hdc in each st around. (18 sts)

Rnd 5: *[Hdc in next 2 sts, hdc 2 in next st]; rep from * around, end hdc 2 in last st of previous round. (24 sts)

Rnd 6: Hdc in each st around. (24 sts)

Rnd 7: Hdc in each st around, sl st in next st, and turn. (Hdc 24 and sl st 1)

BODY OF SLIPPER

Row 8: Ch 2 (counts as first hdc), hdc in each of next 14 sts, sl st in next st, and turn. (Hdc 15, sl st 1)

Row 9: Ch 2 (counts as first hdc), sk sl st, hdc in each st across, including the starting ch-2 of Row 8. Turn. (16 sts)

Rows 10-17: Ch 2, hdc in each st across, turn. Note: To adjust size of slipper add or subtract rows here to desired size. (16 sts)

Row 18: Ch 2, hdc 1 in st at the base of the ch 2. Hdc in the next 14 sts, hdc 2 in the final hdc, and turn. (18 sts)

Row 19: Ch 2, hdc in each st across, and turn. Note: You are increasing the edges for the heel by putting 2 extra sts at each edge. (18 sts)

Row 20: Ch 2, hdc 1 in st at base of ch 2, hdc in next 16 sts, hdc 2 in final hdc, and turn. (20 sts)

Row 21: Ch 2, hdc in each st across, and turn. (20 sts)

HEEL OF SLIPPER

Row 22: Ch 2, hdc in first 5 sts, *[hdc2tog, hdc in next st]; rep from * 2 times. Hdc in last 6 sts, and turn. (17 sts)

Row 23: Ch 2, hdc in first 2 sts, *[hdc2tog, hdc in next st] and rep from * 3 times. Hdc in last 3 sts. (13 sts)

Row 24: Ch 2, *[hdc2tog, hdc in next st] and rep from * 3 times. Note: You should end with a hdc in the last st—the "ch 2" from Row 23. (9 sts)

Join the heel of the slipper with a sl st in the ch-2 sp of Row 24. This will form a small hole in the end of the slipper, the "pull up helper," which helps pull the slippers over your heel quickly and easily. If you don't like the hole, you can simply stitch it up using a small piece of yarn and the tapestry needle after you've finished the slipper.

EDGING AND STRAP

Ch 2, starting on one side (right or left) of the slipper, hdc around the entire slipper edge, sl st to first ch-2 to join. Choosing one edge of the slipper (try starting on the left side with the heel of the slipper facing toward you), ch 1, sc 4 around border, sc2tog, sc 3, ch 17 (this forms the strap). Hdc in third ch from hook, ch 1, sk next ch (this forms the button hole), hdc down rest of chain, sc on slipper edge, and sc2tog. *[Sc 4, sc2tog]; rep from * around the rest of slipper edge. Once you reach your original ch 1, sl st the edging together. Tie off and weave in the ends. (On the other slipper, start the sc edging on the opposite edge so that the straps end up on opposite sides of each other and the buttons face outward.)

FLOWER

Using your accent color, leaving a long tail of yarn, ch 2 and turn.

Rnd 1: In second ch, sc 12 to form a circle of stitches, and sl st to first sc to join rnd.

Rnd 2: *[Ch 4, sk 1 sc, sc in next st]; rep from * around to form 6 loops. Sl st to first ch of beg ch-4.

Rnd 3: [Sc 1, hdc 1, dc 2, hdc 1, sc 1] in each loop of Rnd 2 to form the flower petals. Sl st in first sc 1 of first petal to join. Tie off and weave in ends.

FINISHING

Sew the flower onto the toe on the same side as the button faces using the long tail of yarn and a tapestry needle. Using the tapestry needle and another long strand of yarn in the same color as the flower, stitch on the edging by looping the yarn into each st of the edging. Sew on button and rep pattern for second slipper.

VARIATIONS

* Add a felt or suede sole to make each pair a little more durable.

* Make a teensy pair and gift to a mama-to-be at your next baby shower.

* Simplify by skipping the flower embellishment, or adorn with a premade silk or fabric flower.

JESSICA HARRIGFELD

SAUGERTIES, NEW YORK

After graduating from college with a degree in pre-med/biology, Jessica began knitting, weaving, and crocheting. "During my last year of school, I so desperately wanted to skip classes to stay home and complete whatever project I was working on. So, at the end of the school year, it wasn't really a decision about what I would do," she says. Soon, though, reality set it. "After going broke from spending all of my money on cashmere yarn, I decided that I needed to make it my job to share my art with others," she says. And that she did. She now works out of a 100-year-old artist's studio/home in the woods near Woodstock.

"I learned to crochet at a young age from my Nana, who used to make afghans," Jessica remembers. "She taught me the process, and with a little imagination, I realized that the possibilities with the medium are infinite."

FIND JESSICA
Adventuresofjr.etsy.com   Twitter.com/adventuresofjr

Delicate and soft cashmere matches the feel and style of these ultrafeminine gloves. Make them as a treat for yourself, or for someone in your life who deserves a little special treatment, and consider them a super-simple way to add a touch of luxe to everyday life.

MATERIALS

Yarn A: 3 oz/85 g (50 yd/oz, so approximately 150 yd/141 m)
8 ply Jade Sapphire Mongolian cashmere yarn (shown in Tuscan Sunset)

Size I/9/5.5 mm crochet hook

Yarn B: 3 yd/3 m 4 ply Jade Sapphire Mongolian cashmere yarn
(shown in Tuscan Sunset)

Size H/8/5 mm crochet hook

Scissors

Eight ¾-in/2-cm buttons

Sewing needle

Matching sewing thread

Iron

Gauge: 16 dc and 7½ rnds = 4 in/10 cm

CUFF

(make two)

With Yarn A, ch 22.

Row 1: Dc 1 in the second chain from the hook and in each chain to the end of row. (20 dc) Ch 2 and turn.

Row 2: Dc 1 in each dc to the end of the row. (20 dc) Ch 2 and turn.

Rows 3-12: Rep Row 2.

Row 13: Dc 1 in each dc to the end of the row. (20 dc) Ch 1 and turn.

Row 14: Sc 1 in each of the first 3 dc; *[ch 2, then sk 2 dc, sc 1 in each of the next 2 dc]; rep from * twice more; ch 2, sk 2 dc, sc 1 in each of the next 3 dc. (12 sc and 4 ch-2 sp) Ch 2 and turn.

Row 15: Dc 1 in each of the next 20 sc and ch across row. (20 sts) Do not fasten off.

RIGHT MITTEN

HELPFUL HINT

To help yourself keep track of where you are, mark the beginning of each round. You are working in a spiral unless otherwise noted.

Rnd 1:

❶ Lay 1 cuff piece on a flat surface with the beginning row on your right, Row 15 on your left, and the last st of Row 15 at the top, farthest away from you.

❷ Form the cuff by folding the right edge over and then folding the left edge over so Rows 14 and 15 overlap Rows 1 and 2.

❸ Reinsert your hook into the loop left from the end of Row 15. Sc 3 evenly into the edge of both Rows 14 and 15 and Rows 1 and 2. Continue around top edge by making another 21 sc. Continue to crochet in the rnd. (24 sts)

Rnd 2: Dc 1 in each of the next 12 sc. Dc 4 in each of the next 2 sc. Dc 1 in each sc to the end of the rnd. (30 sts)

Rnd 3: Dc 1 in each dc to end of rnd. (30 dc)

Rnds 4-5: Rep Rnd 3.

Rnd 6: Dc 1 in each of the next 13 dc. Sk the next 6 dc. Dc 1 in each dc to end of rnd. (24 dc)

Rnd 7: Dc 1 in each dc to the end of rnd. (24 dc)

Rnds 8-13: Rep Rnd 7.

Rnd 14: Sc2tog across rnd. (12 sts)

Rnds 15-16: Rep Rnd 14. Make one sl st into the next sc. Fasten off, leaving a 6-in/15-cm tail and weave it into each of the remaining sts.

RIGHT THUMB

Rnd 1: Pick up and begin crocheting in the rnd on the side of Rnd 6 and then the sts left from Rnd 5. Sc 1 on the side of Rnd 6. Continue along side of Rnd 6 evenly making 4 dc. Dc 1 in each of the next 5 dc. (10 dc)

Rnd 2: Dc 1 in the next sc. Dc 1 in each dc to the end of the rnd. (10 dc)

Rnd 3: Dc 1 in each dc to the end of the rnd.

Rnds 4-6: Sc2tog across rnd. Make 1 sl st into the next sc, fasten off leaving a 6-in/15-cm tail, and weave the tail through the remaining sts. Fasten off securely.

LEFT MITTEN

Rnd 1:

① Lay 1 cuff piece on a flat surface with the beginning row on your left, Row 15 on your right, and the last stitch of Row 15 at the top, farthest away from you.

② Form the cuff by folding the right edge over and then fold the left edge over so Rows 14 and 15 overlap Rows 1 and 2.

③ Reinsert your hook into the loop left from the end of Row 15. Crochet along the top edge by making 21 sc. Sc 3 evenly into the edge of both Rows 14 and 15 and Rows 1 and 2. Continue to crochet in the rnd.

Rnd 2: Dc 1 in each of the next 10 sc. Dc 4 in each of the next 2 sc. Dc 1 in each sc to end of rnd. (30 st)

Rnd 3: Dc 1 in each dc to end of rnd. (30 dc)

Rnds 4-5: Rep Rnd 3.

Rnd 6: Dc 1 in each of the next 11 dc. Sk the next 6 dc. Dc 1 in each dc to end of rnd. (24 dc)

Rnd 7: Dc 1 in each dc to end of rnd. (24 dc)

Rnds 8-13: Rep Rnd 7.

Rnd 14: Sc2tog across rnd. (12 sts)

Rnds 15-16: Rep Rnd 14. Make 1 sl st into the next sc. Fasten off, leaving a 6-in/15-cm tail and weave into each of the remaining sts. Pull tight and make a knot.

CONTINUED

LEFT THUMB

Rnd 1: Pick up and begin crocheting in the rnd on the sts left from Rnd 5. Sc 1 in the first dc. Dc 1 in each of the next 5 dc. Dc 5 along side of Rnd 6 dcs. (10 sts)

Rnd 2: Dc 1 in next sc. Dc 1 in each dc to end of rnd. (10 dc)

Rnd 3: Dc 1 in each dc to end of rnd.

Rnds 4–6: Sc2tog across rnd. Make 2 sl st into the next sc, fasten off, leaving a 6-in/15-cm tail, and weave tail through the remaining sts. Pull tight and make a knot.

SCALLOP EMBROIDERY
(for both cuffs)

1 Use H hook and Yarn B and be sure to pull the yarn taut after each st. Holding yarn at the back (inside) of the cuff, make 5 sl st into the tops of the first 5 dc of Row 13 of the cuff.

2 Make 2 sl st into Row 14 directly above last st.

3 Make 1 sl st back down into the same hole as the last st in Row 13.

4 *[Make 1 sl st into the tops of each of the next 4 dc of Row 13.

5 Make 2 sl st into Row 14 directly above last st.

6 Make 1 sl st back down into the same hole as the last st in Row 13.]

7 Rep from * twice more.

8 Make 1 sl st into the tops of each of the next 3 dc of Row 13. Fasten off.

FINISHING

Check to be sure that all tails are woven in, then sew buttons onto the cuffs between Rows 1 and 2 (according to where the button holes are). Block mittens and lay flat to dry. Press with a warm iron to set the stitches.

VARIATIONS

* Simplify by skipping the embroidery on the scallops.

* Cover your buttons with a pretty patterned fabric—like one from Liberty of London.

* Make the body of the glove and the cuff in different, but coordinating colors.

This hat uses repetition to enhance its simple form, which is embellished with a bow that mimics the shape of the pattern. It may be the perfect accessory to celebrate the chilly weather of both the early fall and early spring.

MATERIALS

3 oz/85 g (50 yds/oz, so approximately 150 yds/137 m) worsted weight organic cotton yarn (shown in Gray)

Size J/10/6 mm crochet hook

Scissors

One 3-by-1½-in/7 ½-by-4-cm piece soft lambskin

Sewing needle

Matching sewing thread

One 20-mm pin back

Iron

Gauge: 2 pattern repetitions and 6 rnds = 4 in/10 cm

This hat is worked in the round starting from the crown. Note that the stitch counts do not include chain stitches. There should be a chain stitch between each cluster of 3 double crochet.

Ch 4; join with a sl st in first ch to form a ring. Ch 2. Do not turn.

Rnd 1: *[Dc 3 into the center of the ring, ch 1]; rep from * 4 more times. Join with a sl st into the top of the first st of the rnd. Ch 2. (15 sts)

Rnd 2: Dc 3 into the last ch st of Rnd 1. *[Ch 1, sk 3 dcs, dc 3 into the next ch, ch 1, dc 3 into the same ch]; rep from * 3 more times. Ch 1, sk 3 dc, dc 3 back into the last ch of Rnd 1. Ch 1, join with a sl st into the top of the first dc of the Rnd. Ch 2. (30 sts)

Rnd 3: Dc 3 into the last ch st of Rnd 2. *[Ch 1, sk 3 dcs, dc 3 into next ch, ch 1, dc 3 into same ch]; rep from * 8 more times. Ch 1, sk 3 dcs, dc 3 back into the last ch of Rnd 2. Ch 1, make one sl st into the top of the first dc of the Rnd. Ch 2. (60 sts)

Rnd 4: Dc 3 into the last ch st of Rnd 3. *[Ch 1, sk 3 dcs, dc 3 into next ch, ch 1, dc 3 into same ch]; rep from * once more. **[Ch 1, sk 6 dcs, make 3 dcs into next ch, ch 1, dc 3 into the same ch]. Rep from ** 7 more times. Ch 1, sk 6 dcs, dc 3 back into the last ch of Rnd 3. Ch 1, make 1 sl st into the top of the first dc of the Rnd. Ch 2. (66 sts)

Rnd 5: Dc 3 into the last ch st of Rnd 4. *[Ch 1, sk 6 dcs, make 3 dcs into next ch, ch 1, make 3 more dcs into same ch]. Rep from * 9 more times. Ch 1, sk 6 dcs, dc 3 back into the last ch of Rnd 4. Ch 1, make 1 sl st into the top of the first dc of the rnd. Ch 2. (66 sts)

Rnds 6-12: Rep Rnd 5 seven more times, or until hat measures 8 in/ 20 cm from the beg. Fasten off and weave in tails.

LEATHER BOW

❶ Hold leather piece with the right side facing you and the long sides at the top and bottom.

❷ Make 3 horizontal pleats and hold in place with your fingers. Turn piece over and, using your needle and thread, cinch the pleats together and run the thread through several times to make sure it's secure.

❸ Without tying off your thread, securely attach your leather bow to the pin back using the thread. Fasten off.

FINISHING

Block hat and lay flat to dry. Press with a warm iron to set the stitches. When dry, attach the bow to one side of the hat.

VARIATIONS

* Switch out the leather bow for one made of fabric or ribbon.

* Thread a ribbon through the row above the scallops and tie a bow slightly off of center in front.

* Try a variegated yarn and simplify by skipping the bow.

JOLANTA BEINAROVICA

GRAVENDALE, LATVIA

"I love to experiment with textures, sizes and materials," explains Jolanta, who lives in the Latvian countryside. "For the Linen Lariat, I took the largest hook I have and the thinnest linen thread and started to make simple chains." Her natural aesthetic (cool neutrals, tone-on-tone adornments) is influenced by the calm of her surroundings—sandy beaches, green forests, many rivers and lakes, all hardly touched by civilization in her country, which borders the Baltic Sea. "There is a little piece of my home-land in every one of my creations," she says, of her work, which is influenced by her grandmother and her sister, who were great craftswomen and crocheters.

"I wish to highlight the natural color of linen through my work, to help people see the beauty of natural materials. Sometimes, natural gray is so much more full of energy than any other bright color," notes Jolanta.

FIND JOLANTA
Magdalinen.etsy.com   Magdalinen.erayo.com

Delicate chain stitches lift ordinary thread to a whole new level of delightfulness in this unique project. With the addition of handmade (but easy-to-make) flowers, this necklace is an impressive statement that even a newbie can master.

MATERIALS

1¾ oz/50 g (approximately 600 yd/475 m) natural gray linen thread

Size H/8/5 mm crochet hook

Scissors

Sewing needle

Matching sewing thread

Polyester fabric scraps

Candle

Pliers or tweezers (optional)

Several 3-mm and 6-mm round metallic beads

NECKLACE

1 Make a simple crocheted ch—keeping your stitches loose, delicate, and lacy—of approximately 10 to 12 ft/3 to 3½ m. There's no need to make each ch perfectly identical to the next; the necklace looks more interesting if they are all a bit different in size.

2 Carefully take the ch and make 8 layers in the shape of the necklace. Each layer is approximately 17 in/43 cm long. Hand-stitch the layers together at both ends using the thread.

3 For the tie closure, make 2 linen thread braids, each approximately 15 in/38 cm long, with 4 to 6 strands of thread in each of the 3 sections. Knot at both ends and leave 1 to 2 in/2.5 to 5 cm of threads hanging off of each end. Hand-stitch 1 end of each braid to the ends of the necklace and either tuck the end threads into the ch, or trim them once the braid is securely attached.

FLOWERS

1 To make your petals, take the polyester (or any synthetic fabric that melts nicely) and cut out circles of different sizes up to 1 in/2.5 cm in diameter. Using the candle flame, carefully melt the edges of each circle and gather each one in the middle a little bit to make the shape of a flower. Hold the fabric with pliers or tweezers if you find that to be helpful.

2 Sew the 3-mm beads into the center of each flower using a needle and thread. Carefully hand-stitch the flowers to the crocheted layers.

FINISHING

Stitch the 6-mm beads randomly onto the chain for additional embellishment. To wear, simply tie on the necklace with a bow.

VARIATIONS

∗ Use a lobster closure with an extension chain instead of the braid closure to simplify.

∗ Try playing with colors, using a different shade for the chain than the braid.

∗ Go bolder with your fabric choices to make the flowers really pop, or try using a pretty floral or striped fabric.

Ready to wear as a long and free-form necklace, a headband, or even a belt, this one project will add many accessorizing options to your wardrobe. Tiny petals crocheted throughout the length of this project elevate it above the expected.

MATERIALS

3½ oz/100 g (1311 yd/1200 m) natural gray linen thread

Size E/4/3.5 mm crochet hook

Scissors

1 To start making the floral arches, ch 6 and join with 1 tr to form the first arch. *Ch 2, tr 1 in the starting ch to form the second arch. Ch 2, tr 1 in the starting ch to form the third arch. Ch 1 and turn.

2 Make the petals. (Note: All stitches are worked around the base arches rather than attaching to individual stitches within the arch.)

First petal: Sc 1, dc 1, tr 3, dc 1, sc 1.

Second petal: Sc 1, dc 1, tr 3, dc 1, sc 1.

Third petal: Sc 1, dc 1, tr 3, dc 1, sc 1, and finish the last petal by sc 1 in the individual st at the middle of the arch ch.

3 Continue with a simple ch of ch 21, tr 1 in sixth ch from the hook to form the first arch.

4 Rep all from the * in Step 1 through the end of Step 3. Make about 45 clusters for a lariat approximately 3 yd/3 m long. Cut and tie off to finish. Tie the ends together and wrap on as you like.

VARIATIONS

* Make your lariat as long or as short as you like according to how you plan to wear it.
* Try working in different colors of threads, or even different tones, to give it a more dimensional look.
* Use this method to make a simple necklace with a clasp closure.

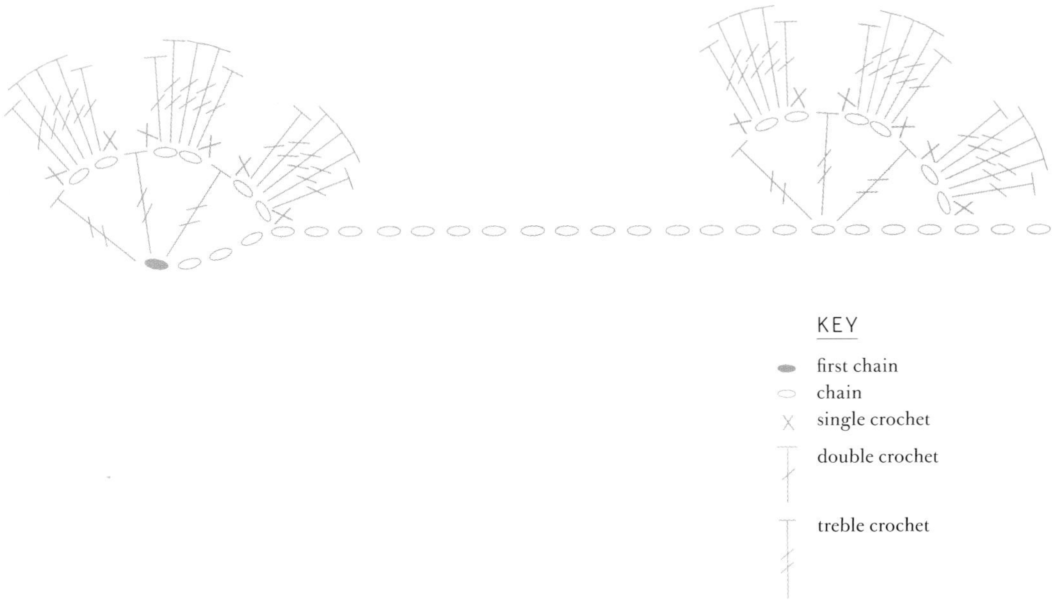
KEY
first chain
chain
single crochet
double crochet
treble crochet

MERCEDES TARASOVICH-CLARK

BIRMINGHAM, ALABAMA

After majoring in fibers and textiles in art school, Mercedes focused on knitting, crochet, hand spinning, and dyeing fibers and teaching dyeing workshops in the Birmingham area. Soon, dyeing and designing became her full-time gig and she set up shop in an outbuilding on her property (hence her company's name, Kitchen Sink Dyeworks). "I'm super fussy about how I lay colors down on the yarn. To me, it really is painting, and it results in a very balanced palette of colors in the finished skein," she says. Her precision translates into her crochet work too, which shows her dexterity with design and her skill for transforming a simple medium into something quite decadent.

"I never know where I might find a great idea, so I always keep my camera and sketchbook handy," says Mercedes. "I have a little Flickr addiction, and I'm always exploring others' photo pools for striking colors."

FIND MERCEDES
Kitchensinkdyeworks.com   Twitter.com/mercedesksd

RUFFLED BUTTON-UP POUCH

Ruffles, as every girl knows, are happiness inducing. Tuck money, notes, keys, or other small items inside this pouch and transform even your morning rush into a cheerful occasion. Or, use it inside of a larger bag to keep odds and ends contained and delight in your newly organized self.

MATERIALS

FOR MULTI-COLOR PURSE:
MC 90 yd/82 m Kitchen Sink Dyeworks Merino Fine in Dexter (gray)

CC1 25 yd/23 m Kitchen Sink Dyeworks Merino Fine in Memphis (seafoam)

CC2 15 yd/14 m Kitchen Sink Dyeworks Merino Fine in Niblette (pink)

FOR SINGLE-COLOR PURSE:
130 yd/119 m Kitchen Sink Dyeworks Merino Fine in Memphis (seafoam)

Size C/2/2.75 mm crochet hook (or size needed to obtain gauge)

Scissors

Tapestry needle

Sewing needle

Matching sewing thread

One ½-in/1.25-cm button

One 5½-by-11-in/14-by-28-cm piece lightweight woven fabric

Steam iron

Finished size: approximately 5½ in/14 cm square
Gauge: 11½ sts and 9 rows = 2 in/5 cm in hdc

The front panel is constructed as a circular crocheted medallion, and then squared off on final round. To work the crocheted ruffles, you work one round through the front loops only of the previous round to create the 3-D surface embellishment, and then a second round through the back loops only to create the sturdy fabric base that backs the panel. For the multi-color purse, you will cut yarn and attach a new color on the back, and for the single-color purse, you will create a short chain that will carry your yarn to the back of the work, where you will attach it to begin the new round.

MULTI-COLOR PURSE

FRONT PANEL

With CC1, ch 10 and join into ring with a sl st.

Rnd 1: Ch 6 (counts as first tr, ch 2) [tr, ch 2] 11 times, then join with a sl st to the fourth st of beg ch-6. Cut yarn and fasten off. (12 tr, 12 ch-2 sp)

Rnd 2: With MC, fasten yarn into first ch-sp just after starting ch. Ch 3 (counts as dc), dc 2 into ch-sp, ch 1, [dc 3 into next ch-sp, ch 1] 11 times, then join with a sl st to the third st of beg ch-3. (48 sts)

Rnd 3: Ch 4 (counts as dc, ch 1), dc into the same ch as join, then working *into front loops only*, [dc, ch 1, dc] into each st of Rnd 2. Join to the third st of beg ch with sl st, cut yarn, and fasten off. (144 sts)

Rnd 4: With CC2, fasten yarn to the back loop of first st of Rnd 2. All sts of this rnd will be worked tbl of Rnd 2. Ch 3 (counts as dc), dc into same st, dc into each of next 3 sts. [Dc 2 into next st, then dc into ea of next 3 sts] to end of rnd. Join to third st of ch with a sl st. (60 sts)

Rnd 5: Ch 4 (counts as dc, ch 1), dc into same ch as join, then working *into front loops only*, [dc, ch 1, dc] into each st of Rnd 4. Join to the third st of beg ch with sl st, cut yarn and fasten off. (180 sts)

Rnd 6: With CC1, fasten yarn to the back loop of first st of Rnd 4. All sts of this rnd will be worked tbl of Rnd 4. Ch 3 (counts as dc), dc into same st, and dc into each of next 4 sts. [Dc 2 into next st, the dc into each of next 4 sts] to end of rnd. Join to the thrd st of ch with a sl st. (72 sts)

Rnd 7: Ch 4 (counts as dc, ch 1), dc into same ch as join, and then working *into front loops only*, [dc, ch 1, dc] into each st of Rnd 4. Join to the third st of beg ch with sl st, cut yarn and fasten off. (216 sts)

Rnd 8: With MC, fasten yarn to the back loop of first st of Rnd 6. All sts of this rnd will be worked tbl of Rnd 4. Ch 3 (counts as dc), dc into same st and dc into each of next 5 sts. [Dc 2 into next st, then dc into each of next 5 sts] to end of rnd. Join to third st of ch with a sl st. (84 sts)

Rnd 9: Ch 1, [sc into each of next 12 sts, ch 12, and sk 9 sts] 4 times. Join to first ch with a sl st. (96 sts)

Rnd 10: Ch 1, [sc into next 12 sc, (sc 6, hdc, dc, ch 2, dc, hdc, sc 6) into ch space] 4 times. Join to first ch with a sl st. (120 sts)

Rnds 11–13: Ch 1, (sc in each st to ch sp, [sc, ch 1, sc] into ch sp), and join to first ch with sl st. Cut yarn and fasten off. (4 sts inc each rnd)

BACK PANEL

Ch 32, hdc into second ch from hook, and each ch to end. (31sts)

All rows: Ch 2, hdc into first st and each st to end.

Work in pattern until piece measures 4¾ in/12 cm or ¼ in/6 mm less than width of front panel. Cut yarn and fasten off.

BUTTON FLAP

With MC, make magic ring: Wrap yarn clockwise around your finger twice to form a loose ring. Insert hook into ring, yo, and draw up loop. Working t-ch and ch 2, hdc 4 into ring, and close ring by pulling gently on the tail (leaving no hole). Ch 2 and turn.

Rnd 1: Hdc 2 into each st, ch 2, and turn. (8 hdc)

Rnd 2: [Hdc 2 into st, hdc into next st] 4 times. Ch 2 and turn. (12 hdc)

Rnd 3: [Hdc 2 into st, hdc into next 2 sts] 4 times. Ch 2 and turn. (16 hdc)

Rnd 4: [Hdc 2 into st, hdc into next 3 sts] 4 times. Ch 2 and turn. (20 hdc)

Rnd 5: [Hdc 2 into st, hdc into next 4 sts] 4 times. Cut yarn and fasten off. (24 hdc)

Rnd 6: With CC2, ch 2, [hdc 2 into st and hdc into next 5 sts] 4 times. Ch 2 and turn. (28 hdc)

Rnd 7: [Hdc 2 into st, hdc into next 6 st] 4 times. Cut yarn and fasten off. (32 hdc)

Rnd 8: With CC1, ch 2, [hdc2 into next st and hdc into next 7 st] 4 times. Ch 2 and turn. (36 hdc)

Rnd 9: [Hdc 2 into next st, hdc into next 8 st] 4 times. Cut yarn and fasten off. (40 hdc)

Rnd 10: With MC, ch 2, [hdc 2 into next st and hdc into next 9 sts] 5 times. Ch 1 and turn. (44 hdc)

Rnd 11: Sc into each of next 20 sts, ch 4, sk next 4 st, sc into each of next 20 st and ch 1. Do not turn.

Rnd 12: Work 1 row of rsc along flap edge. Cut yarn and fasten off.

Fold over the button flap to see where the hole lines up and securely sew on your button using a needle and thread.

CONTINUED

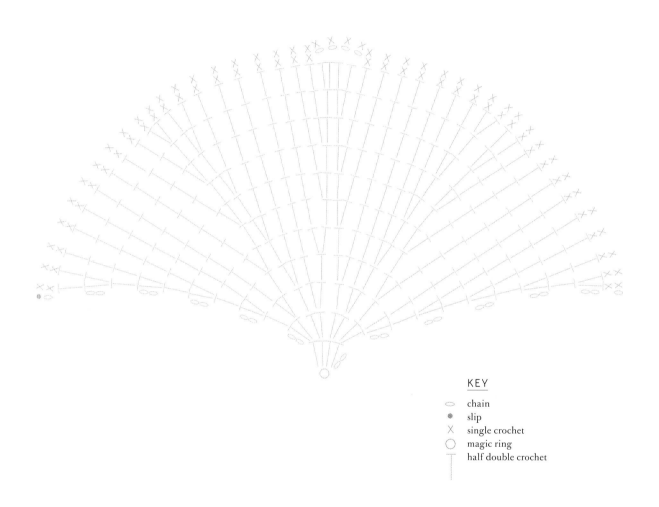

KEY

- ⬭ chain
- ⊛ slip
- ✕ single crochet
- ◯ magic ring
- ⊤ half double crochet

SINGLE-COLOR PURSE

FRONT RUFFLE PANEL

Rnd 1: Ch 6 (counts as first tr, ch 2), [tr, ch 2] 11 times. Join to fourth st of ch with a sl st. (12 tr, 12 ch-2 sp)

Rnd 2: Ch 3 (counts as dc), dc 2 into ch sp, ch 1, [dc 3 into next ch-sp, ch 1] 11 times. Join with a sl st to the third st of beg ch-3 ch. (48 sts)

Rnd 3: Ch 4 (counts as dc, ch 1), dc into same ch as join, then working *into front loops only*, [dc, ch 1, dc] into each st of Rnd 2. Join to the third st of beg ch with a sl st. (144 sts)

Rnd 4: All sts of this rnd will be worked tbl of Rnd 2. Ch 3, insert hook into back loop of first st of the rnd, ch 3 (counts as dc), dc into same st, and dc into each of next 3 st. [Dc 2 into next st, then dc into each of the next 3 sts] to end of rnd. Join to the third st of ch with sl st. (60 sts)

Rnd 5: Ch 4 (counts as dc, ch 1), dc into same ch as join, then working into front loops only, [dc, ch 1, dc] into each st of Rnd 4. Join to third st of beg ch with sl st. (180 sts)

Rnd 6: All of this rnd will be worked tbl of Rnd 2. Ch 3, insert hook into back loop of first st of the rnd. Ch 3 (counts as dc), dc into same st, dc into each of next 4 sts, [Dc 2 into next st, then dc into each of next 4 st] to the end of rnd. Join to 3rd st of ch with sl st. (72 sts)

Rnd 7: Ch 4 (counts as dc, ch 1), dc into same ch as join. Working *into front loops only*, [dc, ch 1, dc] into each st of Rnd 4. Join to the third st of beg ch with a sl st. (216 sts)

Rnd 8: All sts of this rnd will be worked tbl of Rnd 2. Ch 3, insert hook into back loop of first st of rnd, ch 3 (counts as dc), dc into same st, dc tbl into each of the next 5 sts, [dc 2 into next st, dc into each of next 5 sts] to end of rnd. Join to the third st of the ch with a sl st. (84 sts)

Rnd 9: Ch 1, [sc into each of next 12 st, ch 12, sk next 9 sts] 4 times. Join to first ch with a sl st. (96 sts)

Rnd 10: Ch 1, [sc into next 12 sc, (sc 6, hdc, dc, ch 2, dc, hdc, sc 6) into ch space] 4 times. Join to first ch with sl st. (120 sts)

Rnds 11-13: Ch 1, [sc in each st to ch space, (sc, ch 1, sc) into ch sp]. Join to first ch with sl st. Cut yarn and fasten off. (4 sts inc each rnd)

BACK PANEL

Follow directions for Multi-Color Purse.

BUTTON FLAP

Make magic ring: Wrap yarn clockwise around your finger twice to form a loose ring. Insert hook into ring, yo, and draw up loop. Working t-ch and ch 2, hdc 4 into ring, and close ring, gently pulling on tail, leaving no hole. Ch 2 and turn.

Rnd 1: Hdc 2 into each st, ch 2, and turn. (8 hdc)

Rnd 2: [Hdc 2 into st, hdc into next st] 4 times. Ch 2 and turn. (12 hdc)

Rnd 3: [Hdc 2 into st, hdc into next 2 sts] 4 times. Ch 2 and turn. (16 hdc)

Rnd 4: [Hdc 2 into st, hdc into next 3 sts] 4 times. Ch 2 and turn. (20 hdc)

Rnd 5: [Hdc 2 into st, hdc into next 4 sts] 4 times. Ch 2 and turn. (24 hdc)

Rnd 6: [Hdc 2 into st, hdc into next 5 sts] 4 times. Ch 2 and turn. (28 hdc)

Rnd 7: [Hdc 2 into st, hdc into next 6 sts] 4 times. Ch 2 and turn. (32 hdc)

CONTINUED

Rnd 8: [Hdc 2 into next st, hdc into next 7 sts] 4 times. Ch 2 and turn. (36 hdc)

Rnd 9: [Hdc 2 into next st, hdc into next 8 sts] 4 times. Ch 2 and turn. (40 hdc)

Rnd 10: [Hdc 2 into next st, hdc into next 9 sts] 5 times. Ch 1 and turn. (44 hdc)

Rnd 11: Sc into each of next 20 sts, ch 4, sk next 4 sts, sc into each of the next 20 sts, and ch 1. Do not turn.

Rnd 12: Work 1 row of rsc along flap edge. Cut yarn and fasten off.

Fold over the button flap to see where the hole lines up and securely sew on your button using a needle and thread.

FINISHING

(all versions)

Block pieces to finished measurements. Weave in all ends. With WS held together, MC yarn and ruffle front piece facing, join top of button flap to ruffle front piece with 1 row of sc. Holding back piece together with front, continue sc join in same manner along other three sides. Join to first st with sl st, ch 1, and do not turn. Work 1 rnd of rsc around all four sides. Cut yarn and fasten off. Weave in ends.

FABRIC LINING

Fold lining fabric in half crosswise and press. Fold, press, and then sew a ¼-in/6-mm seam along both edges using matching thread and sewing needle. Press both seams to one side of lining, and fold over top edge to ¼-in/6-mm depth and press. Insert lining into pouch with pressed seams facing back and sew in place with whipstitch or sl st seam. Tack pouch front to liner with small stitches, if desired.

VARIATIONS

* Skip the button flap and attach two lengths of pretty ribbon on either side of your pouch for a tie closure.

* Try a zipper secured to the fabric lining in place of the button flap.

* Cover the button with fabric for an even more unique look.

A thick bracelet that's perfect to wear with a simple tank top and shorts, or a summer dress, the pattern of the cuff will inspire you to move beyond a simple granny square. Plus, the sophisticated button closure will make you look polished (even if you don't feel that way).

MATERIALS

40 yd/36.5 m Kitchen Sink Dyeworks Merino Fine in Memphis (seafoam), Dram (toffee), or Valencia (peach) for each cuff

Size C/2/2.75 mm crochet hook (or size needed to obtain gauge; you may want to go slightly smaller)

Scissors

Tapestry needle

Steam iron

Sewing needle

Matching sewing thread

Two ½-in/12-mm buttons

Finished size: approximately 7½ in/19 cm long by 2¾ in/7 cm wide
Gauge: 13 sts and 6½ rows = 2 in/5 cm in dc, after blocking

The cuff is constructed as a circular crocheted medallion, and then each side of the button band is worked flat off of the two opposite sides of the center piece.

CUFF

Ch 8 with your desired color, then join into ring with a sl st.

Rnd 1: Ch 4 (counts as tr), tr 2 into ring, ch 5, [tr 3 into ring, ch 5] 3 times. Join to the fourth ch of the starting ch with a sl st. (32 sts)

Rnd 2: Ch 4 (counts as tr), tr into next 2 sts, [ch 3, tr into ch-sp, ch 3, tr into ch-sp, ch 3, tr into each of next 3 sts] 3 times, ch 3, tr into ch-sp, ch 3, tr into ch-sp, ch 3, and join to third ch of starting ch with sl st. (56 sts)

Rnd 3: Ch 1, [work in sc in each st and ch-sp to corner ch-sp, sc, ch 1, sc into ch-sp] 3 times. Join to first ch with a sl st. (56 sts)

Rnd 4: Ch 1, [work in sc in each st to corner ch-sp, sc, ch 1, sc into ch-sp] 4 times. Join to first ch with a sl st. Cut yarn and fasten off. (60 sts)

BUTTON BAND

With RS facing you, join yarn at any corner and then ch 3 (counts as dc), dc 16 across edge, ch 3, turn (17 sts). [Dc in each st to the end of the row, ch 3, and turn]. Work the preceding row 12 times total, or to desired length. Cut yarn and fasten off.

BUTTONHOLE BAND

With RS facing, join yarn at opposite corner, work as for button band for 2 rows, or to desired length. Ch 1 and turn. For the last row, sc 2, [ch 3, sk 3 sts], for buttonhole, sc 7, [ch 3, sk 3 sts] for buttonhole, end sc 2.

BORDER

Work 1 rnd of sc around the cuff and join to first st of rnd with a sl st. Cut yarn and fasten off.

FINISHING

Steam-block cuff to finished measurements and weave in ends. Using a sewing needle and thread, sew buttons in place to correspond with the buttonholes.

VARIATIONS

* Make the medallion a different color from the button band.

* Sew a folded piece of ribbon where the button would go and use to tie a bow closure through the buttonhole.

* Try a variegated or metallic yarn for a cuff.

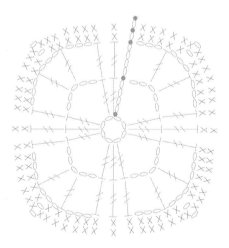

KEY

⌒ chain
● slip
X single crochet

┃ half double crochet

┃ double crochet

┃ treble crochet

EMILY UGOLINI

CORONA, CALIFORNIA

"I first learned how to crochet at a very young age from my Italian grandmother. She worked out of her home, making crocheted dresses, women's skirts and jackets, and beautiful bedspreads and tablecloths," explains Emily, who put down her crochet hook as a teenager because it just wasn't the cool thing to do. "But as life's stresses started to take their toll, I found a comforting refuge in crocheting," she notes. Emily's crochet—which includes jewelry, gloves, and home accents like bowls and coffee-cup cozies—is sophisticated, yet straightforward, and she frequently crochets with thread to mirror the look of doilies and tablecloths.

"I can say with all sincerity that this is no longer my grandmother's crochet," Emily remarks.

FIND EMILY
Nothingbutstring.etsy.com   Twitter.com/nothingbtstring

Simple and sweet, this ring stitches up super fast, and proves that crochet belongs on your finger. In fact, you might find yourself being a bit friendlier, waving at passersby just to show off your hand. Stitch these up for all your friends, and don't forget to make one for yourself.

MATERIALS

Approximately 10 yd/9 m (size 10) Cléa crochet thread in lime green

Approximately 2 yd/2 m (size 10) Cléa crochet thread in bright light green

Approximately 2 yd/2 m (size 10) Cléa crochet thread in olive green

Size 7/4.5 mm crochet hook

Scissors

Matching sewing thread

Sewing needle

RING BAND

Row 1: Using lime green, ch 6, turn.

Row 2: [Sk first st, sc 1 in the next 5 sts, ch 1 and turn].

Rep Row 2 until band is desired length. Do not fasten off.

RING BAND EDGING

Turn band 90 degrees, work 1 row of sc in row ends evenly across. Fasten off, leaving a 6-in/15-cm tail. Join the thread to the other long side, work as for first side. Fasten off, leaving a 6-in/15-cm tail.

Join short ends, using the two tails in a criss-cross stitch to complete.

CIRCLE

Rnd 1: Using lime green, ch 5, join with a sl st to form a ring.

Rnd 2: Ch 1, work 8 sc into ring, ch 1, join to first sc.

Rnd 3: Using bright light green, sc 2 in each sc around. (16 sc)

Rnd 4: Using olive green, *[sc 1 in next sc, sc 2 in next sc]; rep from * around. (24 sc)

Fasten off and weave in end. Use sewing needle and thread to attach the circle to the band, placing the circle on the seam to hide it.

VARIATIONS

* Adorn the center of your circle with a tiny decorative button.

* Use variegated thread rather than multiple colors.

* Skip the circle altogether and enjoy the simple stitched ring band on its own.

I-cord is a hollow crochet tube, sort of like a straw, that gets easier to make the more you do it. Making three and braiding them together results in a pleasing dimensionality (and durability) in this bracelet.

MATERIALS

Approx 20 yd/18 m *total* (size 10) Cléa crochet thread in lime green, bright light green, and olive green

Size 7/4.5 mm crochet hook

Split-ring stitch marker (optional)

Sewing needle

Matchinig sewing thread

Toggle clasp
(available at a craft or jewelry supply store)

Scissors

You'll be making one I-cord in each of the three colors. The first five rows are the most difficult because you are forming the tube of the I-cord. As the I-cord starts to take shape, the work will become easier.

I-CORDS

(make 3)

Using first color, leaving a 6-in/ 15-cm tail, ch 5, join with a sl st to form a ring.

Rnd 1: Ch 1, work 5 sc into ring. Place a marker or a piece of colored thread in first sc to mark the beginning of round. (5 sc)

Rnd 2: * Working in the sts from Rnd 1, with your hook inserted from the center outward, sc 1 in each sc around; move the marker to the next row. You will be working in a spiral; do not join at the end of each rnd.

Continue as for Rnd 2 until I-cord measures the desired length for your wrist, plus a bit extra to accommodate the braid. Double check as you work that there are 5 sc in each rnd—if you deviate from this, the I-cord will either become too thick or too thin, and any mistakes will multiply as the I-cord grows.

Fasten off, leaving a 6-in/15-cm tail.

Repeat from *, using remaining 2 colors.

FINISHING

Sew the three I-cords together on one end and loosely braid them together. Once braided, sew the other three ends together. Using a toggle attachment, sew the ring onto one end and the bar onto the other end using the tails you left while making the cords.

VARIATIONS

* Make your cords longer and braid up a necklace.

* Make the cords in contrasting colors to make a bolder bracelet.

* Use a metallic thread to create a dressier version.

CARA

COREY

RICHMOND, CALIFORNIA

As a freelance writer who focuses on crafty and creative people, Cara balances computer time with creating knit and crochet items. "Some of my biggest sellers have been crocheted fingerless gloves and striped scarves, so I'm almost always working on something with my hooks," she says. With a style that's simple, modern, and casual, Cara doesn't bother with anything too fancy or frilly. "Partly, I don't have the patience for overly complicated patterns, and partly, I love stripes and color blocks, so that's what I make," she explains. Plus, as a Midwestern girl in the San Francisco Bay Area, Cara stays true to her roots with patterns that are very practical. "I love making scarves and hats that are warm enough to hold up to those cold Midwestern winters!"

"I don't think I can have any kind of balance in my life without some kind of creative outlet," muses Cara.

FIND CARA

Marymarieknits.etsy.com   Caracorey.com   Twitter.com/notcarol

By elevating an ordinary object—a simple wooden hanger—above the expected, you can treat your closet to a little handmade love. The possibilities for color combinations in this project are endless, so make a few in colors that you love and get ready to be newly inspired to get dressed in the morning.

MATERIALS

1 skein each (5 oz/140 g and 236 yd/212 m) Lion Brand 100% cotton yarn in Seaspray (A), Poppy Red (B), Natural (C), and Espresso (D)

Size G/6/4.25 mm crochet hook

Scissors

Tapestry needle

Three 17-in-/43-cm-wide vintage wooden hangers

Gauge: Three shells = 4 in/10 cm

You'll need to make two of the shell pieces for each hanger.

SHELL PIECES

With color A, ch 55 loosely.

❶ Dc into the third ch from the hook (counts as 2 dc), dc 3 into the same ch (5 dc-1 shell).

❷ Sk 1, sc 2 into the next ch, *[sk 1, dc 5 into the next ch, sk 1, sc into next ch]; rep from * across, end last rep with dc 5 in last ch. (14 shells)

❸ Turn piece to work along opposite side of ch.

❹ Dc 5 into same shell-sp as previous shell, sk 1, sc into the next ch, sk 1, dc 5 into the next ch (same ch as shell on opposite side); continue in this manner across, ending with dc 5. Join with a sl st into the top of the first dc of the first row. Cut yarn, fasten off and weave in ends. Rep to make another.

ASSEMBLE THE PIECES

❶ Top edge: Place the 2 pieces RS together. Starting at the right-hand side, using color B, join with a row of sc across one long edge, working into 1 st from each piece to join; make sure both sides line up perfectly.

❷ When the top edge is finished, place the cover over the wire part of the hanger, poking the hanger through the backside of the cover.

❸ Continue the sc edging around the bottom of the hanger. (It may help to pinch the two sides together as you work.) When you get back to where you started, join with a sl st into the first sc. Cut yarn, fasten off, and weave in ends.

Rep for 2 more hangers, using color C with A trim and color D with C trim.

VARIATIONS

* Make monochromatic covers for a unified look.

* Make them smaller to fit baby hangers and give them as a sweet handmade gift.

* Use a finished hanger as a display device on a wall.

The inherent shape of granny squares makes for an excellent starting point for creating throw pillows— and for practicing your stitching if you are a beginner. Plus, this project crochets up so quickly that you'll want to make a few to brighten up sofas, beds, and armchairs throughout your house.

MATERIALS

1 skein each (3½ oz/100 g and 77 yd/162 m)
Stitch Nation Bamboo Ewe yarn in Beach Glass (A),
Periwinkle (C), Twilight (D), Lipstick (E), Geranium (F),
Snapdragon (G), Mermaid (H)

2 skeins (3½ oz/100 g and 77 yd/162 m) Stitch Nation
Bamboo Ewe yarn in Mercury (B)

Size I/9/5.5 mm crochet hook

Scissors

Tapestry needle

One 16-in/40-cm square pillow form

GRANNY SQUARE FRONT

Rnd 1: With color A, ch 4. Join with a sl st to form a ring. Ch 3 (counts as first dc, dc 2 into the ring, *[ch 2, dc 3 into the ring (corner 2)]; rep from * 2 times (4 corners total). Join with a sl st into the top of the first ch-3.

Rnd 2: Sl st across the next 2 dc until you reach the first ch-2 corner space. Ch 3 (counts as first dc), dc 2 into the corner space. Ch 2, dc 3 into the same corner space, ch 1. In the next corner space *[dc 3, ch 2, dc 3], ch 1; rep from * for the remaining 2 corners, join with a sl st as for Rnd 1. Sl st to the ch-2 corner space. Now that you have a little square, you're going to repeat this pattern with subsequent rnds, adding more groups of dc 3 between the corners.

Rnd 3: Dc 3 into the corner sp, ch 2, dc 3 into same sp, ch 1. Dc 3 into the ch-1 sp, ch 1, then work the next corner [dc 3, ch 2, dc 3, ch 1 in corner sp]. Continue this way for all subsequent rnds, joining at end of each rnd.

To join new colors, pull the new color through the last loop of your final sl st and begin using that color with the first ch-3 of the rnd; cut the old color, leaving enough yarn to weave in later.

COLOR SEQUENCE

Rnds 1 and 2: A

Rnds 3 and 4: B

Rnds 5 and 6: C

Rnd 7: D

Rnd 8: E

Rnd 9: F

Rnd 10: G

Rnd 11: A

Rnd 12: H

Rnds 13 and 14: B

Fasten off. Weave in all ends on wrong side of the piece.

BACK SIDE

With color B, ch 56. Hdc into the third ch from hook (counts as first hdc). Hdc 55 across for a total of 55 sts. Ch 2 and turn (t-ch counts as first st). Hdc into second row, hdc across. Continue hdc until you have 5 rows. Join D on the last st of Row 5 and work Row 6 in sc. Join B on last st of Row 6, and continue working in hdc for Rows 7–11. Work this pattern (5 rows hdc with B, 1 row sc with D) until piece measures 16 in/40 cm tall. Cut yarn, fasten off, and weave in ends.

ASSEMBLY

Place the 2 squares WS together. Starting at any point with B, sc around three edges, working into sts from both sides to join. Insert your pillow and continue sc along the fourth side. When you get back to your starting point, join with a sl st into the first sc. Cut yarn, fasten off, and weave in ends.

VARIATIONS

* Simplify by making the back with one color.

* Change up the colors on the front according to your preference.

* Add a crochet flower or other embellishment to the center of the granny square.

RAE
RITCHIE

MINNEAPOLIS, MINNESOTA

After making all of her clothes in high school through an almost obsessive interest in sewing, Rae went on to focus on apparel design at university. Now, she works as an accessories designer at a local retailer. "During my career, I was lucky enough to take a trend trip to Japan and was immediately inspired by the simple and delicate care taken in curating and celebrating the small things in life. I think about the look and feel of those small, rustic, and almost pioneer-like boutiques every day," she explains. That comes through in her approach to crochet, where she loves to mix fibers, shapes, and applications as a celebration of the craft.

"I have always loved needlecrafts and the vintage ladylike mood that they convey," says Rae. "Plus, working with crochet is so flexible, and has a delicate look that is contrasted well with rustic materials."

FIND RAE

Reraeshop.etsy.com   Reraeblog.blogspot.com

Using a relatively small hook to make these bowls—which are handy storage for things like fruit, jewelry, business cards, and yarn skeins— makes them strong and sturdy. If you'd prefer a softer bowl that's slightly easier to make, try a slightly larger hook.

MATERIALS

1 skein each (3½ oz/100 g and 180 yd/165 m)
Knit One Crochet Too 2nd Time Cotton (75% Cotton/25% Acrylic)
in Earth (#855), Linen (#810), and Natural (#115)

Size D/3/3.25 mm crochet hook

Scissors

Finished size: Large bowl approximately 3¾ in/9.5 cm tall by 5 in/12.5 cm diameter; medium bowl approximately 3 in/7.5 cm tall by 4 in/10 cm diameter; small bowl approximately 2½ in/6.5 cm tall by 3 in/7.5 cm diameter

As each row is worked, pull on the finished work horizontally to set the stitches. When finished, pull on the work vertically to give a taller appearance.

LARGE BOWL

With Earth, ch 5, join with a sl st to form a ring.

Rnd 1: Ch 2 (counts as sc), sc 11 in ring, join with a sl st into second ch of beg ch-2. (12 sc)

Rnd 2: Ch 2, sc into same st as join, sc 2 in each sc around, join as for Rnd 1. (24 sc)

Rnds 3-4: Ch 2, sc into same st, *[sc 1 into next sc, sc 2 into next sc]; rep from * around to last sc, sc 1 in last sc, join. (54 sc)

Rnd 5: Ch 2, sc into same st as join, *[sc 1 into next 3 sc, sc 2 into next sc]; rep from * to last 3 sc, sc to end, join. (68 sc)

Rnds 6-8: Ch 2, sc in each sc around, join. (68 sc)

Rnd 9: Ch 2, *[sc into next 3 sc, sc 2 into next sc]; rep from * to last 3 sc, sc to end, join. (84)

Rnds 10-15: Ch 2, sc in each sc around, join. (84)

Rnd 16: Ch 4 (counts as dc, ch 1), *[sk 1 sc, dc in next sc, ch 1]; rep from * around, join with a sl st into third ch of beg ch-4. (42 dc, 42 ch-1 sp)

Rnd 17: Ch 2, *[sc into ch-1 space, sc in dc]; rep from * around, join. (84 sc)

Rnd 18: Ch 2, sc in each sc around, join. (84 sc)

Rnd 19: *[Ch 2, sk next sc, sl st into next sc]; rep from * to end to create a scallop finish, join with a sl st into first ch of beg ch-2. Fasten off and weave in ends.

MEDIUM BOWL

With Linen, ch 5, join with a sl st to form a ring.

Rnd 1: Ch 2 (counts as sc), sc 11 in ring, join with a sl st into second ch of beg ch-2. (12 sc)

Rnd 2: Ch 2, sc into same st as join. Sc 2 in each sc around, join as for Rnd 1. (24 sc)

Rnd 3: Ch 2, sc into same st as join. *[Sc, sc 2 into next sc]. Rep from * to last sc. Sc, sl st into second ch from beg. (36 sc)

Rnd 4: Ch 2, sc into same st as join. *[Sc next 2 sc. Sc twice in next sc.] Rep to last 2 sc. Sc to end. Sl st into second ch from beg. (48 sc)

Rnds 5 and 6: Ch 2, sc around, join. (48 sc)

Rnd 7: Ch 2, *[sc next 3 sc, sc 2 times in next sc]. Rep from * to last 3 sc, sc to end, join. (59 sc)

Rnds 8-12: Ch 2, sc around. Sl st into second ch from beg. (59 sc)

Rnd 13: Ch 4 (counts as dc, ch 1), *[sk 1 sc, dc in next sc, ch 1]. Rep from * around, slip into third ch. (30 dc, 30 ch-1 sp)

Rnd 14: Ch 2, *[sc into ch-1 space, sc into dc]. Rep from * around. Sl st into second ch. (60 sc)

Rnd 15: Ch 2, sc around. Sl st into second ch from beg. (60 sc)

Rnd 16: *[Ch 2, sk next sc, sl st into next sc]; rep from * around, join with a sl st into first ch of beg ch-2. Fasten off and weave in ends.

SMALL BOWL

With Natural, ch 5, join with a sl st to form a ring.

Rnd 1: Ch 2 (counts as sc), sc 11 in ring, join with a sl st into second ch of beg-ch. (12 sc)

Rnd 2: Ch 2, sc into same st as join. Sc 2 in each sc around, join as for Rnd 1. (24 sc).

Rnd 3: Ch 3, dc into same st as join. *[Dc, dc 2 in next st]. Rep from * around to last dc. Dc to end. Slip into third ch from beg. (36 dc)

Rnds 4–5: Ch 2 and sc in each sc around, join. (36 sc)

Rnd 6: Ch 2, *[sc 1 into next 3 sc, sc 2 into next sc]. Rep from * to last sc, and sc to end, join. (44 sc)

Rnds 7–10: Ch 2, sc around, join. (44 sc)

Rnd 11: Ch 4 (counts as dc, ch 1), *[sk 1 sc, dc in next sc, ch 1]; rep from * around, join with a sl st into third ch of beg ch-4. (22 dc, 22 ch-1 sp)

Rnd 12: Ch 2, *[sc into ch-1 sp, sc into dc]; rep from * around, join. (44 sc)

Rnd 13: *[Ch 2, sk next sc, sl st into next sc]; rep from * around, join with a sl st into first ch of beg ch-2. Fasten off and weave in ends.

VARIATIONS

* Play with the scale of the yarn and hook, such as trying a chunkier yarn for a more textured final result.

* Use a variegated yarn for an easy way to add multiple layers of color to each bowl.

* Make a bigger set of bowls by expanding the patterns out and in.

Whether it's the holiday season or not, these darling ornaments can liven up any space. Try them in clusters, fastened onto ribbon for a garland, or on their own hanging in windows.

MATERIALS

1 skein each (0.18 oz/5 g and 27.3 yds/25 m) DMC Cotton Pearl
(size 5) (100% Cotton) in Very Light Blue Green (#504),
Coral (#351), and Light Beige Gray (#822)

Size J/10/6 mm crochet hook

Scissors

Stiffy Fabric Stiffener by Plaid Enterprises, Inc.
(available at most craft stores)

Protective gloves

1 tsp/5ml water

Scrap towel

DIAMOND ORNAMENT

With Very Light Blue Green, ch 6, join with a sl st to form a ring.

Rnd 1: Ch 2, sc in ring, *[ch 9, sc 2 in center of ring]; rep 6 times, ch 3, tr in second ch of beg ch-2 to make last loop. (8 loops)

Rnd 2: Ch 4 (counts at first tr), [tr 3, ch 3, tr 4] in the same loop (first corner), ch 5, *[sk next 9-ch loop, (tr 4, ch 3, tr 4) in following loop, ch 5]; rep from * around, working 4 total corners, join with a sl st into fourth ch of beg ch-4.

Rnd 3: Ch 2, sc into next 3 tr, [sc 2, ch 2, sc 2] into ch-3 space, sc into next 4 tr, ch 3, and slip into ch-5 sp and skipped ch-9 loop from previous rows to join together with a sl st. Ch 3, *[sc into next 4 tr, (sc 2, ch 2, sc 2) in next ch-3 space, sc next 4 tr, Ch 3, and slip into ch-5 sp and skipped ch-9 loop from previous rows to join together with a sl st. Ch 3]; rep from * around, Join with a sl st into second ch from beg.

To make the hanging loop, sl st across to first 2-ch loop (corner). Ch 35, join with a sl st into first ch. Fasten off and weave in ends.

LACE ORNAMENT

With Coral, ch 6, join with a sl st to form a ring.

Rnd 1: Ch 3 (counts as first dc), dc 11 in ring, join with a sl st into third ch of beg ch-3. (12 dc)

Rnd 2: Ch 6, *[tr into next dc, ch 2]; rep from * around, join with a sl st into fourth ch of beg ch-6.

Rnd 3: Ch 3, sk next 2 ch, dc in next tr, ch 4, *[yo, insert into last worked st, yo, draw yarn through 2 loops on needle, sk 2-ch space, yo, insert hook into tr, yo, draw yarn through 2 loops, yo, draw yarn through 3 loops, ch 4]; rep from * around, join with a sl st into third ch of beg ch-3.

Rnd 4: Sl st across to center of first ch-4 loop, ch 7, *[sl st into next ch-4 loop, ch 7]; rep from * around, join with a sl st into first ch of beg ch-7.

To make the hanging loop, sl st across to center ch of first ch-7 loop. Ch 35, join with a sl st into first ch. Fasten off and weave in ends.

SNOWFLAKE ORNAMENT

HELPFUL HINT

The picot stitch creates the little nubs on the snowflake.

Ch-3 Picot = Ch 3, sl st into first ch from hook.

Ch-5 Picot = Ch 5, sl st into first ch from hook.

With Light Beige Gray, ch 6, join with a sl st to form a ring.

Rnd 1: Ch 3 (counts as dc), dc 2 in ring, work ch-5 picot, [dc 3, work ch-5 picot] 7 times in ring, join with a sl st into third ch of beg ch-3. (8 ch-5 picots, 24 dc, counting beg ch)

Rnd 2: Sl into next dc, ch 9, sk next [dc, picot, dc], *[tr 1 into next dc, skip next (dc, picot, dc), ch 5]; rep from * around, join with a sl st into fourth ch of beg ch-9.

Rnd 3: *[Ch 4, in 5-ch loop, work (dc 2, ch-3 picot, dc, ch-5 picot, dc, ch-3 picot, dc), ch 4, sl into tr]; rep from * around and join in first st of beg ch-4.

To make the hanging loop, sl st across to next ch-5 picot. Ch 35, sl st into first ch. Fasten off and weave in ends.

CONTINUED

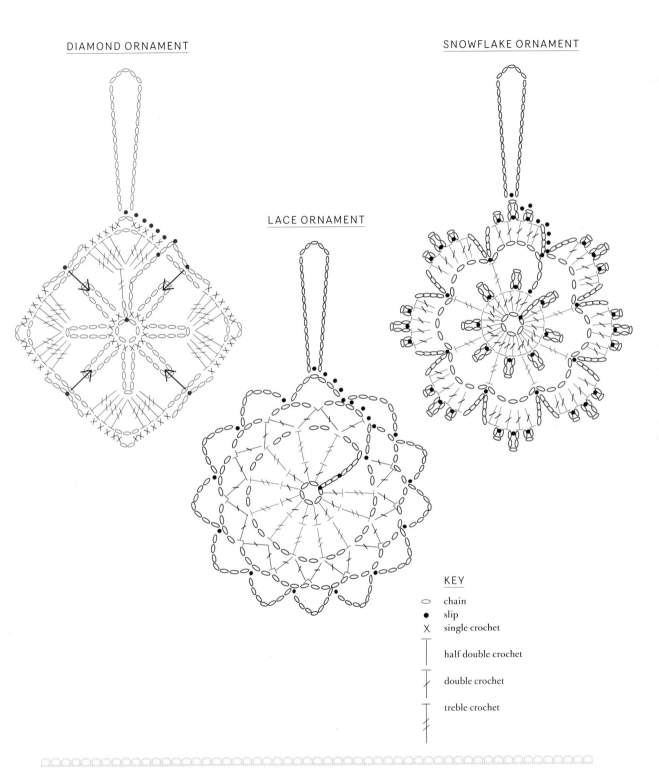

DIAMOND ORNAMENT

LACE ORNAMENT

SNOWFLAKE ORNAMENT

KEY

◯ chain

● slip

X single crochet

⊤ half double crochet

⊤ double crochet

⊤ treble crochet

FINISHING

To stiffen the ornaments, put 2 tablespoons Stiffy Fabric Stiffener into a bowl. Add 1 teaspoon water and mix well. Wearing gloves, dip ornaments into the mixture, fully saturating each, then squeezing away excess. Lay flat on a scrap towel to dry.

VARIATIONS

* Change up the colors according to your preference and consider trying metallic floss.

* Make a handful and turn them into a mobile by hanging them with lengths of thread off of an embroidery hook.

* Use them as gift toppers for an embellishment that will keep giving after the paper is tossed away.

MARIA
RIBEIRO

PALMELA, PORTUGAL

Taking inspiration from the small and beautiful mountain city where she lives, Maria looks to traditions, seasonal food, and even the weather for creative sparks. "I learned to crochet with my grandmother when I was a child and then picked it up again about five years ago," she says. "I practiced the stitches and techniques I remembered and went about learning several more," she continues. With a skill for combining unexpected textural elements, like leather—sourced either locally or from small companies with fair-trade policies—Maria remarks that her intention for these pieces "was to create a light summer version of wool cuffs inspired by beach, light, and timeless surf accessories." A creative person by nature, Maria works as a graphic designer (she describes her work as simple and classic), and fits in her crochet work by managing her time wisely.

"My work is part of the person I am, so naturally, it evolves with me," Maria explains.

FIND MARIA

Kjoo.etsy.com

Inspired by tribal jewelry, this bracelet combines rustic texture with the softness of thread to create a pleasing duality. Wear it on its own as your main accessory, or combine it with other accessories that play on the theme.

MATERIALS

Mercerized cotton thread (size 50)
in multiple colors of your choosing

Steel thread hook slightly smaller than the size
recommended on the thread package
(usually 0.60 to 0.80 mm; using a slightly smaller hook
will keep your stitches tighter)

1 small vintage button

Approximately 10 in/25 cm ¼-in-/5-mm-thick leather cord
(you'll need about 2 in/5 cm longer
than the circumference of your wrist)

X-ACTO knife

Tapestry needle

Each of the three tubes is a seamless piece and you can make the different colored segments as long as you like.

MIDDLE CROCHET TUBE

Work a crochet chain wide enough so that the leather cord just fits inside when folded around the cord; join with a sl st (the first to the last st). Work 2 rnds using sl st and change to sc as you work in other colors. To change colors, work 1 row in sl st, work in the new color, work another row in sl st, and change to sc. Change crochet sts and colors on the same side where the tube started—this side will be the back side. Finish the tube with 2 sl st. Fasten off and weave in ends.

BUTTON TUBE

Make this tube like the Middle Crochet Tube, choosing either the same colors or ones that coordinate. Be sure to make this tube longer than ½ in/12 mm. Sew on the button next to one end, on the good side (the back side will show where you've changed colors). Leave a tail of thread about 12 in/ 30 cm on each tube end.

BUTTONHOLE TUBE

Work another tube the same length as the Button Tube with either the same or similar colors. On one end, work 2 sl st to partially close the tube. Work ch st to the approximate size of the button for buttonhole, work 2 sl sts, closing part of tube on the opposite side. Sl st the ch 2 times to strengthen the buttonhole. Sew up the buttonhole tube tip. Leave a tail of thread about 12 in/ 30 cm on each tube end.

LEATHER CORD

Cut the leather cord to the length needed for a bracelet (just a smidge longer than your wrist— use a bracelet that you like as a size reference if needed). Measure about ⅓ in/7.5 mm from one end and make an incision with your knife no more than about ¼ in/ 5 mm in toward the long side of the leather. Rep on the other end.

FINISHING

Insert the leather cord through the first crochet tube, insert the button tube, and the buttonhole tube. Align the button and the buttonhole tubes on the cord, and with the cotton thread left at both ends, sew the tubes to the leather cord through the incisions on either end.

VARIATIONS

* Stick with a single color of thread, or a few shades that are similar, for a more subdued look.

* To simplify, use softer leather or suede and leave the ends longer so that you can tie the bracelet onto your wrist with a knot.

* Make two or three and wear them together.

One ring is nice, but a set of stacked rings is far better—especially when they feature the unexpected combination of crochet and leather. Decide which finger you plan to wear these on before you start the project to ensure that you size the rings correctly.

MATERIALS

Mercerized cotton thread (size 50) in the colors of your choosing

Thread hook slightly smaller than the size recommended on the thread package (usually 0.60 to 0.80 mm; using a slightly smaller hook will keep your stitches tighter)

1 small vintage button

Approximately 12 in/30 cm ⅛-in-/2.5-mm-thick leather cord

X-ACTO knife

Tapestry needle

CROCHET TUBES

The tubes should be approximately ¼ to ⅜ in/5 to 15 mm in length. Choose your color(s) and length and work a ch wide enough to fit around the leather cord and join with a sl st to first st. Work the length of the tube in sl st, reserving about 10 in/25.5 cm of thread at each tube end. Continue to work four similar tubes.

LEATHER CORD

Cut the leather cord to an appropriate measurement to be the body of the ring (measure against a ring that fits the finger you are making it for).

Measure 1/16 in/2 cm from the tip and cut an incision no more than ¾ in/2.2 cm in the opposite direction. Rep on the other tip.

Rep 3 more times, ending up with 4 of the same-sized pieces of leather cords.

FINISHING

Insert leather cord in the crochet tube, and stitch one end to the other of the leather cord through the incisions. Rep on the other end, making sure to cover incisions with the crochet tube as you seal up the ring. Rep for the other three rings.

VARIATIONS

* Simplify by making just one (or two) rings.

* Use just one color of thread for a monochromatic look.

* Use a length of thread to tie all four rings together so that the crochet tubes line up in a deliberate stack.

PIP

LINCOLNE

MELBOURNE, AUSTRALIA

As a blogger, writer, craft book author, and mother of three, Pip is a busy lady. "I like nice things, but not perfect things," she says. "My Nanna is an amazing crochet queen, as is my Mum, but for some reason I always thought it looked too tricky and never asked them how," she says. "So I learned to crochet at our craft group, Brown Owls, and by following videos on YouTube." Now, she looks to those mums and nannas for inspiration. Her tone is decidedly sweet, with an emphasis on fun and not taking herself, or life in general, too seriously. That outlook comes through in these fun projects, which are endlessly adaptable to your own style.

"It means a lot to me that craft is inclusive and that crafty skills are passed on," says Pip. "I try and help achieve this by sharing my crafty skills and creating updated, modern projects using age-old techniques. I want everyone to make things every day!"

FIND PIP

Meetmeatmikes.blogspot.com   Twitter.com/meetmeatmikes

Bunting is downright lovely, especially when you can easily customize it with any words that you like. Try a festive word, a loved one's name, or a phrase that inspires you. String these up for a nursery, to celebrate a special occasion, or just because.

MATERIALS

One 1¾-oz/50-g ball 8 ply wool/acrylic blend yarn in gray

One 1¾-oz/50-g ball 8 ply wool/acrylic blend yarn in pastel

Size E/4/3.5 mm crochet hook

Scissors

Tapestry needle

Finished size: Triangles will measure around 5 in/13 cm across the top and 5 in/13 cm from top to tip. The bunting will measure 70 in/2 m from end to end.

TRIANGLES

With gray, ch 3.

Row 1: Sc into second ch from hook, sc into next ch, turn. (2 sc)

Row 2: Ch 1, sc into first sc, sc 2 into next sc, turn. (3 sc)

Row 3: Ch 1, sc into first and second sc, sc 2 into last sc. (4 sc)

Rows 4–25: Continue as above, so for every row, ch 1, sc 1 into the first sc, and each sc across to last st, sc 2 into the last st.

You need to crochet 25 rows to complete the triangle. When you are done, sl st to finish and then fasten off securely, leaving a long tail.

To sew in your ends, thread your needle with the loose yarn end and carefully weave it in and out of the stitches to conceal it, first one way, then back the other way. Cut the end very close to your work and give both sides of your triangle a little tug so that the end disappears into the stitches.

LETTERS

❶ Thread your needle with a length of pastel yarn and tie a knot at one end. Carefully cross-stitch your letters onto each triangle of your bunting. Try and keep the letters the same size and as centered as you can. Use your stitches as an imaginary grid for your cross-stitch and remember, it doesn't need to be super perfect.

❷ Tie off the yarn at the back of your triangle and cut the loose end neatly.

TRIANGLE CHAINS

❶ Make the chains to join your bunting triangles by making a slipknot with a long tail on your hook (10 in/25 cm is good). Ch 15, fasten off, leaving a long tail at the end. Rep to make 5 chains like this.

❷ Arrange your letters in the correct order.

❸ Thread the loose end of the ch through your needle and carefully stitch the chain firmly onto one corner of your triangle. Rep for the other loose end of the chain, threading it and stitching it securely to the corner of the adjacent triangle.

❹ When you have stitched things nice and firm, weave the remaining yarn through the st of the triangle a few times. Cut the loose end close to your work to finish. Continue joining your triangles until your word is spelled.

BUNTING CHAIN

❶ Leaving a long tail at the beginning of your work, ch 60.

❷ Make a loop to hang your bunting with by counting back 10 sts and then sl st a couple of times into that tenth st to form a loop.

❸ Fasten off your work and then st the non-loop end of your ch to the corner of the triangle at one end of your bunting. Rep, making another ch with a loop and stitching it to the other end.

❹ Sew in the loose ends by making a few sts into the ch and cutting the yarn.

EDGE THE TRIANGLE

Hdc into each st along the top of the bunting triangles. Cut the yarn and weave in loose ends.

VARIATIONS

* Add tassels to the bottom of your triangles.

* Glue on felt letters for a faster finish.

* Crochet each triangle in a different color.

"Coconut Ice is an Australian confection made from all sorts of things you should not really eat a lot of," Pip explains. "It's a lovely pink and white layered delight, which will make your teeth hurt just from looking at it!" These coasters are an ode to happy teeth and all things pretty and pink.

MATERIALS

One 1¾-oz/50-g ball 8 ply wool/acrylic blend yarn in pink

One 1¾-oz/50-g ball 8 ply wool/acrylic blend yarn in white or cream

Size E/4/3.5 mm crochet hook

Tapestry needle

Scissors

Finished size: approximately 4 in/10 cm in diameter; makes 4

COASTER

For the foundation ring, using pink, make a sl st knot and place it on your hook. Ch 4, then poke your hook into the first ch. Yo and join with a sl st to form a ring.

Rnd 1 (pink): Ch 3 (counts as first dc), dc 11 into the center of the ring, join with a sl st into third ch of the beg ch-3. Fasten off by cutting your yarn around 12 in/30 cm from your hook and pulling the loose tail through the final loop on the hook tightly to form a knot.

Rnd 2: Join new color (white) as follows: Tie new color onto both loops of a st in the previous rnd, insert hook from front to back into the st where the yarn is tied, yo and pull up a loop (i.e., pull yarn through to the front of your work to form a loop), ch 3 (counts as first dc), dc 1 into the base of the st where you joined your thread, dc 2 into every stitch of the previous rnd, join with a sl st into the third ch of beg ch-3. Fasten off, leaving a 12-in/30-cm tail. (24 sts)

Rnd 3: Join pink. Ch 3 (counts as first dc), *[dc 2 into the next st, dc 1 into the next stitch]; rep from * around, ending dc 2 into the final stitch, join with a sl st and fasten off neatly and firmly. (36 sts)

Rnd 4: Join white. Ch 3 (counts as first dc) dc 1 into the next st, *[dc 2 into the next st, dc 1 into the next 2 sts]; rep from * around, ending dc 1 into the final stitch, join with a sl st into the third ch of beg ch-3. Fasten off, leaving a 12-in/30-cm tail. (54 sts)

Rnd 5: Join pink. Sc 1 into each st around. (54 sts) Fasten off neatly.

FINISHING

Thread your needle with the loose tail of yarn. Sew your ends in neatly by weaving the needle between the stitches, pulling the loose yarn through as you go. First weave one way, then the other. Cut yarn close to your work and give your coaster a tug to make the end magically disappear among the stitches.

Repeat to make a whole set of 4 coasters.

VARIATIONS

* Make each coaster in all one color, or in two slightly different shades of the same color.

* Take the coasters up in size and use them as trivets.

* Add a simple edging or weave a length of ribbon through.

WHERE TO SOURCE SUPPLIES

There's nothing quite like standing in front of a wall of vivid and colorful yarn. Here are some of our favorite resources for shopping for the basics, no matter where you live. And remember: Yarn shops are filled with folks who love yarn, which often means they will be happy to share their knowledge.

BROOKLYN GENERAL STORE

Brooklyngeneral.com
128 Union Street
Brooklyn, NY 11231

Catherine Clark and Katie Metzger created Brooklyn General to sell yarn, fabric, notions, and dry goods, including handspun cashmere yarn, to city folk.

CRAZY GIRL YARN SHOP

Crazygirlyarnshop.com
1150 5th Street, Suite 152
Coralville, IA 52241

With two locations, these shops keep the yarn stashes of Iowans full.

DEPTH OF FIELD

Depthoffieldyarn.com
405 Cedar Avenue
Minneapolis, MN 55454

Shop this downtown Minneapolis store for natural yarns and supplies—and be sure to hit their sale loft for bargain skeins.

KNITTED TOGETHER

Knittedtogether.com
7450 Bridgewood Boulevard, Suite 225
West Des Moines, IA 50266

Des Moines' favorite yarn shop is filled with a great selection of yarn, patterns, and notions, and has a comfy area to sit and crochet with friends by the fireplace.

THE KNITTING NEST

Theknittingnestaustin.com
8708 South Congress, Suite 570
Austin, TX 78745

This Texas-style yarn shop goes big in choice, both in yarns and in their offerings of crochet, knitting, dyeing, and Amigurumi classes.

KNITTY CITY

Knittycity.com
208 West 79th Street
New York, NY 10024

This is an Upper West Side institution that's constantly hosting events and book signings to introduce the people behind the yarns and products that they carry.

NINA: A WELL-KNIT SHOP

Ninachicago.com
1655 West Division Street
Chicago, IL 60622

Nina is a zen yarn shop in Wicker Park focused on high-quality yarns and a calm environment.

PURL CITY YARNS

Purlcityyarns.com
62 Port Street
Manchester, MI 2EQ
England

Purl City carries supplies for crocheting, knitting, weaving, and spinning, and also hosts a weekly group to stitch and chat.

PURL SOHO

Purlsoho.com
459 Broome Street
New York, NY 10013

Shop online or visit in person for yarn, notions, and books galore. You might want to pick up some fabric while you're there; their selection is hard to beat.

THE TANGLED WEB

Tangledwebb.com
7709 Germantown Avenue
Philadelphia, PA 19118

A shop with a focus on learning, this shop offers a wide selection of yarn and notions, as well as classes in everything from sock making to crochet and needlepoint.

TWISTED

Twistedpdx.com
2310 NE Broadway
Portland, OR 97232

Owned by Emily Williams and Shannon Squire, Twisted carries locally produced yarn, as well as a wall of sock yarn, and a tea bar.

URBAN ARTS & CRAFTS

www.Urbanartsandcrafts.com
4165 North Mulberry Drive
Kansas City, MO 64116

This store is a crafter's dream come true. With beads, yarn, paper, ribbon, buttons, fabric, and anything you might need in between, this shop has it all.

URBAN FAUNA STUDIO

Urbanfaunastudio.com
1315 16th Avenue
San Francisco, CA 94122

UFS sells independent and sustainable yarn, notions, and craft supplies. They host workshops and rent studio space and equipment (like spinning wheels) by the hour.

WILDFIBER

Wildfiber.com
1453 14th Street, Suite E
Santa Monica, CA 90404

Wildfiber is a large and sunny shop in Santa Monica stocked to the brim with yarn, notions, and how-to materials.

WILD FIBRE

Wildfibreyarns.com
6 East Liberty Street
Savannah, GA 31401

This is a fiber arts and yarn shop where students and grads of the Savannah College of Art and Design (SCAD) go to stock up.

More and more people are taking the time to make high-quality yarns in small batches. Here are some stellar suppliers.

BLUE MOON FIBER ARTS

Bluemoonfiberarts.com

Tina Newton discovered a passion for dyeing her own roving shortly after she started spinning. Now, working with both hand-spun and mill-spun, the company specializes in silk and silk blends and offers a popular sock knitting camp.

BLUE SKY ALPACA

Blueskyalpacas.com

Carrying hand-spun alpaca yarns in high-sheen sport weight, silk, mélange, and a smooth worsted, they also offer bulky alpaca wool and a huge range of worsted cotton colors.

BRIAR ROSE

Briarrosefibers.net

They produce hand-painted yarn in merino, merino and Tencel blends, and wool and flax blends. The company also sells beautiful handmade ceramic buttons.

HELLO YARN

Shop.helloyarn.com

Adrian Bizilia is a trained artist who started making her own yarn over a decade ago. She also offers a fiber club (that runs in three-month installments and usually has a waiting list) where members receive 4 ounces each of her hand-dyed wool or wool-blend fiber yarn.

HIGHLAND HANDMADE

Shop.highlandhandmades.com

A husband and wife duo from Maine sell hand-dyed roving and yarn in subtly variegated colorways.

KITCHEN SINK DYEWORKS

Kitchensinkdyeworks.com

KSD has hand-dyed yarn, patterns, and clubs, including the Badass Yarn Club, where members get a monthly skein of hand-dyed yarn named for a woman who's fighting the good fight. A portion of the fees for the club is donated to a charity of each woman's choosing.

KNIT PICKS

Knitpicks.com

A family-run business based in Vancouver, Washington, Knit Picks is known for high-quality knitting supplies—yarn and needles in particular—at affordable prices.

LION BRAND YARN

Lionbrand.com

This is a commercially available yarn in a wide range of fibers and gauges (including recycled cotton and easy-care Wool-Ease), with in-depth online resources including how-to videos and tutorials.

MALABRIGO

Malabrigoyarn.com

A small, family-owned yarn company, Malabrigo works with a cooperative of women to make a line of colorful and hand-painted yarns.

MOCHA'S FIBER DESIGNS AT TUCKER WOODS FARM

Mochasfiberconnection.com

Kettle-dyed and hand-painted yarns come from Kelly Radding, who started out dyeing yarn from the Pygora goats and llamas on her family's farm. They now offer fifteen different yarn bases and many colorways.

THE PAINTED SHEEP

Thepaintedsheep.com

Kris Granatek offers hand-painted yarns in one-of-a-kind colorways and spinning fiber. They offer a variety of weights of blended yarns using merino, Tencel, and alpaca.

PISGAH YARN & DYEING COMPANY

Peaches-creme.com

With a history that dates back to the 1940s, this North Carolina–based company is one of the last few American textile mills. They produce specialty cotton, rayon craft, and apparel yarns.

SEE JAYNE KNIT YARNS

Seejayneknityarns.etsy.com

Jayne hand-dyes and hand-paints high-quality commercially and hand-spun yarn in merino and merino blends, and sometimes has roving on offer as well.

STITCH AND BITCH YARN

Stitchnationyarn.com

Sheep, bamboo, and alpaca yarns by Debbie Stoller come in a wide range of colors from bright and poppy to soft and neutral.

STRICKEN SMITTEN

Strickensmitten.com

Stocking bright hand-dyed yarn mostly in shades of jewel tones, this shop offers a range of yarn, including one-of-a-kind colorways called "Serendipity Skeins."

THREE IRISH GIRLS

Threeirishgirls.com

What started as a side gig for former high-school teacher Sharon McMahon turned full-time in 2010 with a 3,000-square-foot studio near the shores of Lake Superior. This self-described "yarnista" is passionate about hand dyeing.

WOOL CANDY

Woolcandy.etsy.com

They have nice offerings of hand-dyed yarn and fibers in merino, merino blends, fingering, and silk.

For mixed media crochet projects, here are the go-to spots for beads, ribbons, embroidery thread, buttons, and more.

BUTTON & CRAFT

Coatsandclark.com

This is thick and sturdy sewing thread for securing embellishments (and hand stitching).

DMC

Dmc-usa.com

DMC threads are widely available and useful for embellishing and finishing. The site also features instructional videos and tutorials for everything from crochet to cross-stitch.

FIRE MOUNTAIN GEMS

Firemountaingems.com

A wealth of supplies including seed and bugle beads, crystals, and jewelry supplies including clasps, hooks, and earring and pin bases.

M&J TRIMMINGS

Mjtrim.com
1008 Sixth Avenue
New York, NY 10018

Buttons, buckles, handles, appliqués, and cords make this an excellent place to stop to stock up on crochet accessories.

TINSEL TRADING COMPANY

Tinseltrading.com
1 West 37th Street
New York, NY 10018

Manhattan's finest trimmings shop—which started in the 1930s as an importer of metal thread—features a collection of ribbon, embellishments, paper, tassels, buttons, and floral delights.

WEEKS DYE WORKS

Weeksdyeworks.com

Weeks carries hand-overdyed embroidery floss in a gorgeous spectrum of colors. They also offer hand-dyed wool fabric, sewing thread, and pearl cotton.

Community Supported Agriculture (CSA) is spreading rapidly and there are more and more fiber CSAs in operation. As a member, you'll pay for a portion of the roving or yarn that's harvested each season and will split the harvest with fellow members. Often, you have the chance to specify roving or yarn, in the fiber that you prefer.

CREEKSIDE ACRES
Creeksideacres.com
Pleasant Valley, NY

This Hudson Valley fiber CSA offers tiered options depending on the volume of roving or yarn you're interested in. Shareholders also have the choice of type of fiber—alpaca or Pygora goat.

HATCHTOWN FARM
Hatchtown.com
Bristol, ME

Learn what goes into making fleece and how this sheep farm works, and get a share of yarn or roving in return in the spring.

JACOB'S REWARD FARM
Jacobsreward.com
Parker, TX

Sign up for a share of this Texas alpaca and wool fiber and get a free spinning class to boot.

JUNIPER MOON FARM
Fiberfarm.com
Palmyra, VA

Based in Virginia, this yarn CSA offers a portion of their "yarn harvest" to their subscribers. You can also purchase roving or visit for a farm stay where you can spin in the pasture.

MAPLE VIEW FARM ALPACAS FIBER & YARN CSA
Mapleviewfarmalpacas.com
Brandon, VT

Join this Vermont CSA for a full or partial share and receive a volume of alpaca in either fiber or yarn form in one of two natural colorways.

TOMORROW'S FARM
Tomorrowfarm.net
East Leroy, MI

Get to know the alpacas behind your fiber with a half or full share of yarn or roving. Visit the farm's fiber studio for spinning supplies, spun yarn, and fiber arts classes.

VERMONT GRAND VIEW FARM

Grandviewfarmvt.net
Washington, VT

Join for a 1-lb/455-g share of creamy white mill-spun 2 ply bulky weight Romney-Mohair yarn, receive it in the summer, and have plenty of time to whip up holiday gifts through the fall. You can also purchase their hand-dyed yarn by the skein in their Etsy shop.

WILLOW RIDGE FARM

Faktorwillowridge.com
Lucas, IA

Yarn or roving shares are available (in full or half portions) from the farm's Shetland sheep. Every six to eight weeks, a portion of either 3 lbs/1.4 kg of roving or up to 1800 yd/1650 m of handspun yarn will be delivered to your door.

Getting out and interacting with the folks who raise the animals and provide us with yarn is always a joy. Visit thistlecovefarm.com for a more extensive fiber festival list to find one near you.

IOWA SHEEP & WOOL FESTIVAL

Iowasheep.com
Adel, IA

Educational seminars, a fiber learning center, and plenty of vendors combine with shearing and animal activities during this festival each June.

MARYLAND SHEEP & WOOL FESTIVAL

Sheepandwool.org
West Friendship, MD

Learn to spin and how to properly handle wool at this May festival sponsored by the Maryland Sheep Breeders Association.

NYS SHEEP & WOOL FESTIVAL

Sheepandwool.com
Rhinebeck, NY

This is a yearly festival on the third full weekend in October that features sheep and wool vendors, as well as craft and cooking demonstrations.

SHEPHERD'S HARVEST SHEEP AND WOOL FESTIVAL

Shepherdsharvestfestival.org
Lake Elmo, MN

This forum for wool producers, consumers, and artisans to share and learn from each other occurs each Mother's Day weekend in May.

VERMONT SHEEP AND WOOL FESTIVAL

Vermontsheep.org
Tunbridge, VT

Visit in early October to view the hand-spun wool contest and to stock up on locally produced roving and yarn.

HOW TO FIND INSPIRA-TION

Crocheters love to share their work online. Here's where to find them and where to go to join an online community of your own.

CRAFT YARN COUNCIL

Craftyarncouncil.com

Find resources for professionals and amateurs alike, with detailed instructions on crocheting basics.

CROCHET TODAY

Crochettoday.com

The bi-monthly magazine available at newsstands and craft stores shares tools, tips, patterns, and articles on fellow crocheters.

CUT OUT AND KEEP

Cutoutandkeep.net

This is a site to share tutorials and projects with friends near and far.

INTERWEAVE CROCHET

Interweavecrochet.com

Interweave publishes crochet magazines, as well as online resources including an editor's blog, a shop, and free patterns. Their online community for crocheters can be found at crochetme.com.

KNIT HAPPENS

Knithappens.com

The online community forum of Stitch 'n Bitch, where you can join to do both with other knitters and crocheters.

PINTEREST.COM

Keep track of projects, resources, and inspiration as you travel the web, mood board style.

RAVELRY

Ravelry.com

With well over a million members, Ravelry is a place to keep track of yarns, tools, and projects, and to share your finds with friends. With completely user-driven content, the site is a virtual hub for yarn-related inspiration.

Here are a few places to turn when you're in need of a creative boost.

ALICIAKACHMAR.COM/BLOG

This is an excellent source for free knitting and crochet patterns from Alicia Kachmar.

ATTIC24.TYPEPAD.COM

Lucy crochets in vivid color from her home in the North of England, where she also stays busy sewing, cooking, and gardening.

BLAIRPETER.TYPEPAD.COM

Blair Stocker is the crafty brains behind Wise Craft. Visit for stylishly handcrafted musings.

DORISCHANCROCHET.COM

A peek inside the world of crochet designer Doris Chan.

DOTTIEANGEL.BLOGSPOT.COM

The recycled, vintage, crafty goodness of Tif Fussell never fails to inspire.

MAKESOMETHING.CA

Karyn Valino's online home is a wealth of crafty eye candy.

PICKLES.NO

Patterns for knitting and crochet by Anna and Heidi in Norway. They also sell a lovely range of yarn at shop.pickles.no/no.

ROSYLITTLETHINGS.TYPEPAD .COM

Where stitchery maven Alicia Paulsen blogs about life and creations. Follow to stay in the know about her pattern releases.

SANDRAJUTO.BLOGSPOT.COM

Crochet, illustration, and inspiration straight from Europe-based Sandra Juto.

THECRAFTSDEPT .MARTHASTEWART.COM

The very talented folks of Martha Stewart's craft department share daily inspiration, tools, and projects.

THEPURLBEE.COM

The online channel of Purl Soho, filled with projects and tutorials.

WHIPUP.NET

A crafty forum to share projects with fellow creatives from Australia-based Kathreen Ricketson.

WOODWOOLSTOOL .BLOGSPOT.COM

Ingrid Jansen, popular maker behind Wood & Wool Stool in the Netherlands, shares DIY projects and her latest crochet creations.

WRENHANDMADE.TYPEPAD.COM

Laura Normandin shares her crochet musings among thoughts on art, babies, and general crafts.

Having a small stack of trusted crochet books that you can turn to for inspiration or problem solving is always a good idea.

The Crochet Answer Book:
Solutions to Every Problem You'll
Ever Face; Answers to Every
Question You'll Ever Ask
by Edie Eckman
Keep this small volume on hand to help you troubleshoot patterns and projects.

Crocheting in Plain English
by Maggie Righetti
All the basics of crochet in one place.

Kid's Crochet: Projects for Kids
of All Ages
by Kelli Ronci and Lena Corwin
Projects for mini-mes, including hats, scarves, and friendship cuffs.

Stitch 'n Bitch Crochet:
The Happy Hooker
by Debbie Stoller
From the most basic chain to fancier lace stitches, the book teaches it all, plus gives you a great assortment of projects to create.

ACKNOWLEDGMENTS

This book is dedicated to my grandmothers, Mary and Mildred, who were always making things with their hands. From bridal gowns and veils, to tiny knit hats for newborns, and as many holiday decorations as the house could hold, they taught me to nurture and consider my own creativity. I cherish that I'm able to use their well-worn sewing, knitting, and crochet tools in my own making. I am enormously grateful to the contributors who participated in this book. Victoria, Janelle, Margie, Brandy, Jessica, Jolanta, Mercedes, Emily, Cara, Rae, Maria, and Pip, I am absolutely delighted to share your work and to give others a chance to get to know you each as I have. May you always inspire through sharing your creativity. Many thanks to Joshua Dolezal, Virginia Sole-Smith, Stefanie Von Borstel, Laura Lee Mattingly, Allison Weiner, and the entire Chronicle Books team, for their help in bringing these pages to life.